Codependence and the Christian Faith

CODEPENDENCE
AND THE
CHRISTIAN FAITH

Walter C. Jackson

BROADMAN PRESS
NASHVILLE, TENNESSEE

Unless otherwise indicated, Scripture is from the *Revised Standard Version of the Bible* copyright 1946, 1952, © 1971, 1973 by the National Council of the Churches of Christ in the U.S.A., and used by permission. References marked KJV are from the *King James Version.*

Library of Congress Cataloging-in-Publication Data
Jackson, Walter C., 1933-
    Codependence and the Christian faith / by Walter C. Jackson.
      p.   cm. — (The Bible and personal crisis)
    Includes bibliographical references.
    ISBN 0-8054-5451-9
    1. Codependents—Religious life. 2. Co-dependence—Religious
aspects—Christianity. I. Title. II. Title: Codependence and the
Christian faith. III. Series.
BV4596.C57J33 1990
261.8'322—dc20
                                       90-30195
                                           CIP

To Jackie

Preface

The first purpose of this book is to attempt a simple story of where the label "codependent" came from. The second purpose is to present a composite definition of codependence as it exists as we enter the nineties. Its third purpose is to describe its relationship to a host of other labels and names in the chemical addiction family and other styles of addiction, and to clarify their relationships to each other. This includes listing and giving clear descriptions of symptoms and patterns of codependent life-styles to help readers know what kinds of people are being labeled codependent and what kinds of behavior make up the pattern of codependency.

Its fourth purpose is a rather broad one—that is to make an assessment of these findings from a Christian perspective. That will require giving attention to evidences of codependence in the Bible with some clear references to theological teaching. It will also require at least an outline of the strengths within the Christian faith related to all we are coming to know about codependence. The end result hoped for, of course, is to assist people to discover what the codependents among us look like and to help them to find ways to recover from the damage their codependence brings about to individuals and families.

A final purpose is to address the issue of codependence as it may be present in our churches. The goal here is to use the same help from the biblical and theological sources, as well as counselors and researchers, to suggest ways to avoid the pain of codependent processes and behaviors within the church.

Chapter 1 will state briefly the history of the word *codependence* as it emerged from among alcoholic and substance abuse counselors and researchers. It will highlight the rich information from that source and from the field of addiction studies to shed light on the understanding of codependency as a personality style in reaction to addicts.

Chapter 2 will follow the codependence writers into the field of family studies and there discover the rich new sources of information available about the personality style of the codependent person. Additional varieties of codependent persons will be outlined and new characteristics will be added to the growing definition of codependence.

Chapter 3 will outline a Christian perspective on codependence. Answers will be offered to the following questions: What resources among Christians are available to understand codependency? What does codependency look like from a Christian perspective? What help and assistance is available for Christians who discover they are codependents?

Chapter 4 will outline the process of recovery recommended by the codependency counselors and therapists. It will comment on the usefulness of these methods and processes for all people, especially for Christians.

Chapter 5 will take a brief look at the church as a local "family of God" and suggest ways in which the codependence phenomenon is visible and may be seen to cause problems. Some suggestions for dealing with codependence in the local church are offered.

Chapter 6 will offer a composite definition of codependency with a special focus on the Christian faith.

Acknowledgments

I express my gratitude to those who have aided my research and writing of this book, especially those who have looked to me as a pastor, chaplain, conference leader, pastoral/family counselor, and seminary professor through the years since ordination in 1955. They have been and continue to be my teachers in the areas of addiction and codependence as we have reflected together upon them in our lives.

I thank Broadman for the invitation to investigate codependence seriously and for being understanding during the process of research and writing; and I thank the Sunday School Board for its wisdom in making available informative pastoral literature on timely topics through its Broadman Reader's Plan, the principal sponsor of this volume as well as the twelve-volume personal crisis collection. I am indeed grateful to my esteemed colleague Edward Thornton for his editorial assistance and nurturing skills for novice authors here in Louisville, the city of my residence.

I am grateful to my caring and supportive colleagues Clarence Barton, Michael Hester, Andrew Lester, and Wade Rowatt for their timely encouragement and sustaining friendship before, throughout, and since the period of research and writing. I am also grateful to my enduring friend Wayne Oates whose reading of the manuscript and timely suggestions have been a primary source of challenge and encouragement.

To The Southern Baptist Theological Seminary through its trustees and administrative officers for its generous sabbatical leave policy that provided concentrated research, reflection, and writing time to complete the manuscript, I owe an exceptional debt of gratitude. Beyond the seminary, I owe a great deal to the many faithful Southern Baptists who contribute financially to our denomination to undergird the labor I and my colleague professors invest in serving Christ as ministers of teaching, researching, writing, and preaching through the seminary.

I reserve my warmest and most tender affection to my wife Jackie, to whom this book is dedicated, and to our children, for I have been preoccupied with the production of this manuscript longer than any of us predicted at the outset, and now have finished by the grace of God.

Walter C. Jackson
December 1989

Contents

An Introduction to Codependence

Codependence is a new word to some of you. Your major reason for reading this book, then, may be out of curiosity to learn what it is. *Codependence* is a word others of you have heard before, but you're not sure what it means. You have seen and maybe even looked at one or more of the dozens of books recently written about codependence.

You may have heard people talking about it, attended public lectures about it, listened to pastors mentioning it in sermons, and listened to teachers in schools and colleges using the word. You may have heard people you love and respect speak kindly about the word *codependence* as if it were something good to know about. You may have heard others say some unkind things about it, and you are just confused. You may be reading this book to sort through some of that confusion.

Or perhaps you are like a lot of people who hurt; and you've been hurting for years in ways you don't understand. You have no words to explain your everyday pain. The agony you feel in the very depths of your soul is screaming out for some relief. And now, these people who talk about codependence talk about your aches and pains to illustrate codependence.

Some people get married to each other in a burst of love and affection; and before the end of the first month, they are like strangers living together under the same roof. Have you lived your life with loving and caring people, but now you don't seem to be able to please them no matter what you do? Do you find yourself making up little white lies about almost everything to your mate, children, friends, and then spend your life in terror covering up and trying not to get caught? Have you been married for twenty or more years, but your feelings have been "dead" for a long time? Now you are drifting. You want out; you are tempted to be in a sexual affair with someone else; you find yourself spending money foolishly; you have gained too much weight and don't know why you eat all the time.

When people talk about codependents, it sounds like they're talking about you, or at least about people you know and care about. They surely seem to have known people much like the family you grew up in, and maybe people who make up the family you live in now.

They talk about some things codependent people do to try to make their hurts easier, and they are talking about the things you, your family, and your friends have been doing and trying to do for as long as you can remember. They talk about people who get buried in their work, people who work two or more jobs. They talk about people whose family life suffers because they are deeply invested in some civic club, some moral crusade, or some sport that takes them out of the home. Jobs around the house go half-finished. Apologies are made, promises are given, only to require another round of apologies and promises later. There is no intimacy, almost no friendship or shared activities. Some even try going to church together to regain their lost togetherness, but that does not add any warmth to the home either.

And when the researchers say those things don't work for co-dependent people, and you know they don't work very well for you and for your people either, you wonder if you are codependent.

Many pastors and other ministers who have been trying to make sense out of the trials and tribulations of people in their churches are often confused by the many different struggles they see. They have tried everything they learned in any classroom, in every book, lecture, and conversation they've ever had with chaplains, pastoral counselors, and other helping professionals; but nothing has helped very much. Some ministers are saying the codependence information is most helpful.

Other trusted ministers, counselors, and physicians have said we should be a little cautious about this newly organized information. It has been collected from so many different sources we just can't be sure about whether it will help all that much.

While *codependence* is the word used mostly by counselors and professional "helpers" of many kinds, to most of us the kind of life-style called codependent is not new. If we stop and think about it, something in the many definitions applies to almost all, if not to all, of us at one time or another.

Well, what is it?

Just what is codependence?

I wish there was a simple definition to use. But that's not the case. There are so many different definitions it's impossible to choose one that covers everything. Seven or eight years ago, the word meant something relatively simple. But today it is different. The word has come to mean so many things today that unless you cover a whole page with the definition and use some very technical jargon, you are bound to leave out something very important.

But you have to start somewhere. So I will begin with some partial definitions I have collected from several of the books about codependence. They are given here to get your mind thinking about the subject in a clear way, and I have included some illustrations that may help you to have a better understanding that goes beyond just the words themselves.

Codependence is a dysfunctional way of living life. It is injurious to the person who lives out codependent patterns and to the people around them. First, *it is marked by a behavior where a person*

spends much of the time and energy meeting other people's needs.
This is a kind way of saying they are people who, first and fore-
most, make a habit of being "helpers." Actually, they are not just
helpers in the general sense of helpful, *these are committed, compulsive, "rescuers" who are helpers in spite of whether other people
want to be helped or not.* Most of the time, codependents are not
even aware they are being so hardheaded about being helpers.
They are just helpers all the time when they have a choice about it
and even when they don't think about it.

This is a way to look at codependence from the outside. It's the
kind of definition someone uses when talking about another person who is said to be codependent. A different point of view is to
define what codependence looks like on the inside of a person.
The second definition does that.

A second way to talk about codependence is to say that *it is a
behavior based on the belief that the helper is not worth anything at
all, and the only way the helper can gain value is to meet other people's needs.* Codependence, in this definition, is a way people act
to earn worth or value for themselves, and that way to act is by
meeting the needs of others. They behave as if this kind of behavior is the only possible way to give their life meaning or purpose.
They seem to have no meaning or purpose of their own. So, this
codependent activity is not the ordinary kind of dependence
where persons openly need and want to help someone for a limited time or once in a while for a special purpose. Rather, codependence is the kind of deeply hidden dependency where people live
in pain unless they have someone else to need them. They feel
that they really have no value in and of themselves. They frequently do not take care of themselves physically, mentally, or
spiritually. They are people we refer to in our culture as people
with low self-worth or low self-esteem.

As you might imagine, in the third place, *codependents do not
have the ability to be aware of their own true feelings.* Consequent-

ly, they do not have the ability to be emotionally present to anyone. They are often rather shy people, although sometimes they have learned to be just the opposite. They may perform like the life of the party, but behind all the bluster you do not get any honest or solid feelings. They frequently avoid direct requests for their opinions or feelings about specific matters.

Researchers say codependents are, in the fourth place, *constantly behaving as if they have the ability to control other people, their actions, their feelings, and the processes around them; at least they try to do so by exerting themselves in their most helpful and sacrificial ways.* This is very similar to the childish belief system that if you wish hard enough, or hold your mouths just the right way, you can affect the outcome of the universe.

A fifth characteristic of note is that *codependents are "people pleasers."* In that regard, they seek approval constantly and are extremely sensitive as to whether other people approve of them and their activities. They dress to please or are very embarrassed if they cannot be presentable. They behave in the most proper ways; and they take care of the most minute needs of others, both to satisfy their need to be helpers and to store up credits so as not to be vulnerable. It is in this sense, in the sixth place, that *codependents are considered to be reactors and not actors.* Once outside the area of sacrificial doing for and rescue operations for others, they show little initiative or creativity.

Another part of the inner life of codependents reported by the researchers is *their personality style of avoidance of difficult or unhappy situations by the practice of denial or delusion.* They sense interpersonal storms coming, and then they retreat. If that fails, they revert to some compulsive activity to keep themselves feeling normal. After the fact, they forget or deny it happened. To relieve unhappiness, they use an active fantasy life—the daydream technique—to create an island of peace in which they can live long enough to settle their emotions. Codependents do not have a corner on this activity, but one consistent codependent use of the daydream is to fantasize a story in which they become the heroes.

Of particular interest to Christians is the next characteristic. *Codependents appear either to have onionlike personalities—that is, they have no core values, no firm standards by which they live, and are mostly other-directed; or they have one or more very rigid, unbending core values that they apply to every situation whether it rationally seems to apply or not.*

Another characteristic for this preliminary definition has to do with decisions. *Codependents seem not to know how to make choices.* At least, they do not make choices often or well. They are usually very compliant to authority persons and will be able to fulfill almost any request within the reach of human abilities. They will exhaust themselves to please someone once given the decisions and a direction to follow. Ambivalent choices are confusing to them, and they usually will not make a choice.

Finally, and in an almost paradoxical way, *codependents tend to be perfectionistic;* that is, they insist on performing things exactly as they "should" be done. The "should be" may be derived from a variety of sources. Usually, the drive to perfection follows the lead of the person giving directions for the task at hand. In the absence of that kind of supervision, the codependent will follow the instructions he or she has mentally filed away from some previous authority and do it just that way.

The word *codependence* was developed to have a quick way to talk about people who behaved in these ways. Actually, when you look around carefully, you can see lots of people who seem to fit into the description of the above characteristics.

A clear example is provided by today's parents. Some mothers or fathers find great meaning and purpose in caring for their children. They never cease to be "super moms" or "super dads." I don't mean the normally warmhearted mothers or fathers who love their children and take care of their legitimate dependency needs as they arise. Healthy, godly parents rear their children so they become strong, free, and independent individuals. You know parents like that. Their children grow to adulthood and, of the children's own free choices, they become good friends with their parents. Honestly, some of the most beautiful kinds of relationships in life are the ones that happen between mature children whose parents are considered among their "best friends." Parents are proud of children like this, and they love them as they always have without placing conditions on what children had to do to get that love. Love is free to the child as it always was.

The codependent "mom-child" or "dad-child" relationship is much different. It is rigid and has no warmth. Children of codependent parents have to earn anything they get, even love. Nothing is free. It is a relationship where the father or mother refuses to let the children make decisions, especially important ones, for themselves. They dread to see their children grow up to become free persons. The children never sense being respected, trusted, or loved; they know only what it means to be coerced, controlled, mistrusted, and punished. The children of codependent parents often stay home and never marry because of emotional coercion to stay under mom or dad's control.

Mostly, however, the children move away or marry at the first opportunity. They want to be completely free. However, they still have mom and dad attempting to interfere at every opportunity. Codependent parents are the dad or mom who shows up unannounced, the mom who cannot "abide" the way the child dresses and so sends clothes, the dad who can't stand the child's peers and is always nagging—even after age twenty-five, and the mom who must know the whereabouts and plans of her child(ren) at all times but who is nearly overcome with nervous energy if she or they are off the radar scope. And when the parents are around their adult children, they still treat them like underage children.

Cartoonists have made comical fun of this kind of mom-like or dad-like behavior, giving us categories of a dominating mother or an interfering father-in-law. Actually these characteristics may well be the classic codependent behavior of parents who are persons desperately needing someone to need them.

Unfortunately, the children of codependent parents who escape into early marriages often find they have taken their troubled patterns of living with them. More of mother and dad's way of living has been carried with them than they ever realized. Their problems are compounded by the problems carried into marriage by their mate. Together they more than likely reproduce the dysfunctions of the homes in which they grew up. Many early divorces are the direct result of such codependent behaviors.

Another example is seen in the adult world. Here we see codependents who make God's gift of marriage into an emotional garbage dump. Codependents unconsciously seem to select addicted marriage partners or other "losers." I knew one woman who married and then divorced three physically abusive alcoholic husbands. After three years of single parenthood, she intended to marry a sober, God-fearing man. She dated only Christians she met at church. And only her commitment to God, great personal resolve, and memories of painful beatings by her previous husbands enabled her to give the engagement ring back to the man she had intended to marry when she discovered that he too was an alcoholic. She had "picked him out of a crowd of 150 men at a church singles event" she said. "How did I do it?"

When codependent women marry alcoholics, they can play their helping game, become rescuers to their hearts content, and even become living martyrs. In the process, their lives are lived in misery, their children's lives frequently sustain crippling emotional or physical injuries, and their family's total contribution to society is reduced by massive proportions.

When codependents marry each other, their lives together often become an exercise in cold war tactics until they explode into open sniper fire or full-scale battles. Both partners desperately need to draw meaning from each other by giving to each other. And both are accustomed to gaining their meaning only by giving. Neither is able to receive with warmth. They are both unpracticed in intimate communication. They find they are mostly in pain because they are not getting in marriage what they need or want. When they begin to manipulate, control, or use the other kinds of tactics they have learned from their parents or other adults, they meet with counter-strike warfare from their mates.

Marriage between two codependents becomes a place of daily combat instead of the warm, open, honest, and mutual need-meeting intimate relationship God intended. They divorce each other often and move in and out of marriage frequently because they can't stand to live alone. They create blended families by the trainload, and they set up repeat performances by training their children in the art of codependent relationship styles by their examples.

Love in a codependent marriage is often disguised as "Let me be close to you so I can meet your needs," but the real message is "Let me get near you so I can get my needs met because I have to have someone else to control in order to find myself." Love, codependent style becomes

> impatient and unkind, jealous and boastful, it is constantly arrogant and creatively rude. Codependent love always insists on its own ways; it is irritable and resentful without end. It rejoices when the spouse is wrong because that gives much ammunition for future ambushes, and hates it when the marriage partner is right, because that will mean another weapon for the enemy. In codependent love, nothing is borne unless it will allow one to play the martyr later; nothing is believed because when you grow up with lies, you learn not to trust. Hope has no ground on which to stand—hope is just a fantasy you used to have as a child—and codependent love, yes even codependent love, gets to a place where

endurance fails; codependent love does not continue because it never really began.[1]

Behind the paraphrase of the biblical words, many of you know the kinds of painful, even brutal battles of your own homes. Some people can't even get to church on Sunday mornings without at least three arguments, with wife or husband starting and postponing one or more major arguments from last week and either ordering the children to "shut up" or actually spanking them in the car in the church parking lot. A good pastor friend I know checks out the family barometers in his congregation each Sunday morning by walking through the nursery, preschool, and children's rooms in the Sunday School classes. He listens with his eyes and ears to the children's verbal and nonverbal communications about how things are going at home. He has gotten many accurate pictures of troubled families by this method.

Some of these codependent persons may be friends whom you know and some who attend your church. Some of them may even be members of your extended family. You may even have some people in your own life who relate to you this way. You may relate to someone else like this yourself. If so, a study of codependence may be an important way for you to understand your own needs, as well as a better way to understand the world around you.

This is really not a technical book, however. I hope you won't read this book, then use it to go around looking for people with codependent symptoms so you may label them and use the word to put distance between yourself and them. That would defeat the purpose of gaining information like this. My main goal is to promote self-understanding.

Do you have any symptoms like this? Do these symptoms and symptom patterns help you to see you are in the codependency process? Are you now able to see that your pain is real; that there are trained professionals able and willing to help you find relief for your pain? Are you aware that there are many Christian counselors among those well-trained professionals who themselves are recovering codependents and all the better able to help you on the road to recovery?

If you can answer these questions affirmatively, then the book will have done its most important work.

Then, when you recognize the symptoms, sense the pain and agony of others caused by codependence, perhaps you and other Christian "recovering" codependents can inspire them by your testimony. Tell them about the help you have received. Encourage them to get some help for themselves.

Have you ever heard anyone called a codependent? Or, have you ever heard people calling themselves a codependent? What do they mean? What does it say about the person? How do you treat someone like that? Are they dangerous? Are they good people? What do codependents mean when they say they are "recovering"; that they will never be completely free from it, but they are happy to be recovering? What do some of them mean when they say Christians are religious addicts? Why do many of them say that some kinds of Christians constantly abuse people, especially children? And why do many of them believe Christianity and the church are unable to help people who are codependents? What do they mean when they say the only way to begin to recover is to begin in a profoundly "spiritual" way?

This book is being written to answer these questions, and especially to answer them for Christians.

Notes

1. Author's paraphrase of 1 Corinthians 13:4-8.

1

Where Does the Term Codependence Come From?

It is important to know the history of the development of the word *codependence*. It actually was first applied to people who were married to alcoholics. One of the earliest and clearest definitions of a codependent person is someone who is in a love relationship with an alcoholic. Its roots are found buried with problem drinking and alcoholism, one of the most destructive habits practiced by Americans. It deals especially with the life-styles of individuals and family members who live with or who are in love with problem drinkers and alcoholics. Codependent life-styles developed as people lived with their addicts.

If you have or have had an alcoholic or a heavy drinker in your family, or if members of your family spend large amounts of money and time socializing around beverage alcohol, then you might be glad to know that something good has come from the care and study of alcoholics. The many counselors and helping professionals who have worked with alcoholics are primarily responsible for the discoveries that led to the organization of the codependence materials. They have isolated the many symptoms, the patterns called codependent relating, and have designed many of the initial care and treatment plans related to recovery for codependence.

Before reading further in this book, I want to tell you a true story. It's an account of the life of some of my friends. I will want you to refer to this story as you read later sections in the book, so I hope you will give it some attention. It will serve as a reference guide to understand some of the symptoms of addiction, some of the strategies of codependents, and give you a basic idea of the relationship patterns that develop between alcoholics and codependents in a three-generation family.

The story will especially help you to remember that codependence, like alcoholism, has inheritable parts. It is influenced by heredity. Its features are passed on from generation to generation. All of the researchers have reported this as part of their findings. I have also observed this without exception in the people I have seen in my ministry as pastor, chaplain, and pastoral counselor.

Mary's story is true in the sense that all of its features have happened to real people I have known. In order to disguise the participants, I have taken parts of this story from three different families who do not know each other. However, their separate families illustrate the point that no matter where alcoholics and their codependent family members live, no matter what the major circumstances of their lives, the way they treat each other—the process of their relationships—is almost identical. I have woven the parts of their stories together here because the word *codependence* was first invented to apply to people who were just like them—just like John and Mary and just like their children, just like Mary's mother and her sisters, just like John's father and his brothers. They were all addicts and codependents in the way they related to each other and in the ways they sought to meet their own needs in their relationships with family members.

Mary's Story

Mary is sure something is wrong with her. She has headaches almost every day beginning at 4:30 p.m., just a half hour before she leaves work to go home. The doctor says they are migraine headaches.

Home!

How she is starting to dread going there. If it wasn't for her children, she might have left home years ago; but there she goe⋅ again, losing faith. "Forgive me, dear God," she quickly prays. and gets ready to take her discounted sack of groceries home.

Fifteen years married to a man who drinks is a long, long time.

She wouldn't admit even to herself that John was an alcoholic until six years into the marriage, but everybody knows it now. She still loves him, she thinks; and she will still do anything she can to help him.

John started out so well. He is so bright. Except he's a drunk, just like his father. But she still hasn't given up hope. Not yet, anyway.

Once Mary could conceal his drinking from his coworkers at the office, from some of their friends, and their neighbors. She did this for about seven years.

Even now, John can lie and make almost any new acquaintance believe he has no problems, that he has a perfect marriage and family.

The really bad times come and go. They don't fight now like they used to do. It was horrible when the kids were small. She and John would scream at each other. Now when he starts to drink, she fusses quietly; and he just ignores her.

When he gets drunk now, only her children and sisters help Mary cover for John and clean up his messes. No one invites them to go anywhere with them any more. They have no social life at all. Mary doesn't even cry any more.

Only Mary's sporadic attendance at the church with her children relieves her drudgery. She attends mostly in the warm months, but not the winter because she does not have enough nice winter clothing to go to church. But she refuses to be discouraged. Mary has faced hardships before, and every time she has been able to pull things out. With God's help and by the strength of her own will she has been able to manage all right. But that's her private interpretation.

Their girls, Meg and Jan, are extremely loyal to John; but Mary knows they resent having to alibi for him. They lie routinely about his fake "out-of-town" work and his phony "pneumonia." They're afraid to bring their girlfriends home for fear their dad will embarrass them.

John brags on Meg and Jan, praises them at every opportunity;

but there's no close daughter-dad relationship. They just have a nonaggression pact. The girls love Mary and are sometimes close to her, she thinks. But Mary will not move against their loyalty to their father. They never have talked about what alcohol is doing to them.

Sometimes she wonders what they really think of her. Every time she decides to talk with them about that tender question, she backs away and puts it out of her mind. She loves her girls. They are behaving just like she wants them to behave even without her saying anything. That is enough for now; but Mary would give anything if they would run home from school, hug her neck, and share their day's activities with her. She puts such silly and obviously selfish things out of her mind quickly. She's never there anyway.

Four-year-old Johnny is another story. He still plays "Moms and Dads" by sitting in front of the TV with his can of soda pretending it's beer. He imitates his dad in so many ways it's frightening. He responds to his mother as if she were a jail guard, sometimes calling her "warden." She wonders with terror what will happen when Johnny becomes a teenager. She avoids thinking about that too. She's an ace at putting things out of her mind.

Mary sometimes thinks about her own childhood. Her mother had been an alcoholic. Mary and her sisters had been so ashamed. They would never invite anyone home with them. Often their mother had been so "sick," Mary and her sisters had taken over the household chores—her older sister had taken on the role of mother.

As adults, neither Mary nor her sisters ever tasted a drop of an alcoholic drink. Their baby brother had been a terror, a teenage drunk, and had gotten killed on high school senior prom night in a drunk driving accident.

Their father, on the other hand, had been a kind, quiet, churchgoing man. He waited on their mother hand and foot. He seemed never to get tired of covering up for her when she was drinking. Actually, it was their dad who gave them the only support they ever knew. But even he related to them with distance. How they longed to find someone to love them. They were really set up to fall for the first man who spoke kindly and gave them approval and affection. They all married before they were nineteen years old. And they all married men who were heavy drinkers. Both sisters are in their second marriages, both to new alcoholics.

Mary has already begun to wonder if her girls will suffer the same fate. Even worse, it terrifies her to think that little Johnny might be on his way to an alcoholic life-style.

She is preoccupied each day with ways to make things better for her family. She lives on the hope that one day everything will get better. John will stop drinking, just as he has often said. He has promised a hundred times, but he never keeps the promises for longer than a week or two—that is, not since he had a "born-again" religious experience five years ago. He stayed sober for nine months, until their pastor was called to another church. He was drunk the night after the pastor's moving van left town.

Mary believes, deep in her heart, that she is somehow to blame for much of the sadness in her family and that she must do—even feels driven to do—something to make things better. She is so ashamed of herself and how her family is turning out. She believes she just must try harder and everything will be all right.

But she often gets so rattled she wants to scream out loud. She has so much strength, though, she seems to be able to keep her feelings and frustrations locked inside. She used to be able to find peace when she went to church. But that was when John used to go with her most of the time.

Even the church members have stopped trying to be friends with John. Mary is an object of pity. They speak kindly to Mary when they see her checking groceries at the supermarket, but they wonder how she holds it all together.

Some folk even wonder why she doesn't have a headache all day long.

Some Early Comments on Mary's Story

John is obviously an alcoholic. He is addicted to alcohol. He does not have the power within himself to stop drinking after he gives in to his craving and takes the first drink. He manages to keep his job because he does have some talent, but also because he has been lucky and because Mary has taken care of him. He used to have a very abusive tongue that he let loose on Mary all the time, but then she could give back as good as she got. His vicious tongue is silent now. He and Mary have ceased verbal hostilities. He knows he needs her. Besides, she earns the money to pay most of the bills. This makes him feel very sad, very guilty, and sometimes very ashamed; but he feels these ways only when he is half drunk. Now, when he gets drunk, he just cries himself to sleep.

Mary is a classic codependent personality. She has chosen a husband who, as long as he is an alcohol addict, will need a helper to survive. In order to be an addict and survive, he needs a codependent helper to sustain himself in the manner to which he has become accustomed. Mary takes care of him just like his mother did. She must not think very highly of herself to have accepted such abuse day after day for fifteen years.

Mary is a compulsive helper; she will not stop helping John. She believes she is responsible for all their troubles. She does not know why, but she believes it. If things don't work out, she feels guilty and is ashamed. She believes she has to try harder, and then things will finally get better.

Her mother and father taught her how to live. John's parents taught him how to live. Together they are teaching their three children their patterns. Meg, Jan, and little Johnny are all destined to be adult children of alcoholics, codependents of a special variety.

Codependency as Addiction[1]

Codependency is a word originally designed to describe how people act when they automatically and willingly take care of an addict. The history of the word can be traced back to the work of doctors, nurses, social workers, ministers, psychologists, and other counselors with alcoholics. In their long history of working with alcoholics, they eventually learned the traits of the alcoholic's family members, their need for friendship and support, but more recently became aware of their desperate plight and need for professional attention.

In the process of developing ways to give support and assistance, they began to refer to these persons by a variety of names: coalcoholics, para-alcoholics, near-alcoholics. Eventually, they centered on the label "codependent." At first, the word *codependent* was meant to describe the way people in the families of alcoholics acted toward the addicts themselves. Later, after careful study, the behavior of the nonalcoholic family members came to be seen as the actual way in which some nondrinking family members of alcoholics acted toward everyone.

So a brief glance at alcoholism will be helpful to understand codependence. If codependence is like alcoholism, getting a good review of alcoholism in mind is good preparation to grasp the growing meaning of codependence.

Alcoholism is no respecter of persons. Anyone may become alcoholic. It affects young and old, rich and poor, strong and weak, and persons of all races. In the most ancient cultures, alcoholism was spoken of as a menace to family and community alike. In present-day America,[2] three distinctive patterns of alcoholism have developed: (1) those who drink large amounts of alcohol each day, (2) those who drink heavily only on weekends, (3) those who stay sober for periods of time (weeks or months) and then spend periods of time (weeks or months) in heavy drinking. Two distinctly different patterns may be practiced by all three of these persons as well. The first pattern is called *gamma alcoholism.* Common to the United States, gamma alcoholism is the alcoholism that appears to be able to be controlled by not taking the first drink. However, after the first drink, the alcoholic continues to drink compulsively until broken health, poverty, or being cut off from an alcohol supply ends the episode. This is the pattern of drinking reported by large numbers of alcoholic members of Alcoholics Anonymous throughout this country.

The other pattern is reported from France where a person apparently must drink enough alcohol at least to keep his or her alcohol level up to a certain level. There is no compulsion to raise the level higher or to become "drunk." However, if the person fails to drink the proper amount during the day, then this kind of alcoholic also goes through the standard withdrawal symptoms and other indications of alcoholic addiction.

In some places today you will hear people speak of alcoholism as a personality weakness. Church people usually call it sin. People who believe the personality weakness or sin theories hold that alcoholics have no control over themselves, have a weak character, or are just outright sinners. They use the label "alcoholic" as a term to shut such persons from their minds and responsibilities. They just shake their heads, smack their lips in a "tisk-tisk" fashion, and dismiss the person, their families, and themselves from the problem. This is using a label much as Pontius Pilate used the bowl of water at Jesus' trial, wanting no part of this Galilean. It does provide such people with a self-righteous place to stand. It gives them a judge's bench and whatever joy they can get from being a condemner of sinners. The community of helping professionals in the chemical dependency professions, however, has spent a great deal of time and energy studying alcoholism, the addicts, and their families. By getting close and caring enough to listen to what the alcoholics and their families have to say, they have learned a great deal worth knowing.

Many of them have been teaching that alcoholism is certainly the result of a disease process, with suggestions of genetic influence in the disorder.[3] Those using this theory argue that the disease may be either (1) in the physical body where certain chemical changes occur after a certain amount of alcohol has been consumed, or (2) in the personality structure of people who get to the place that they crave alcohol, becoming psychologically dependent on it and driven to have it.

While the definition of character weakness may apply to some alcoholics, it also seems to be true that alcoholism is a chronic disease with a process. It has predictable stages in which the victim gets progressively worse and may die unless the alcohol intake stops. Effects on the personal life-style of the alcoholic and the ways he or she relates to others in public are the major places society sees the damage of alcohol. The larger and most damaging parts of the disease are the ways in which the entire disease process, both physical and interpersonal, affect the people living most closely to the alcoholic.

Among alcoholism's major characteristics as a disease are the following. Alcoholism

- creates an increased tolerance level in those who become addicted—they really can hold more alcohol than others and, as time goes on, really need more to "get drunk" than others;
- causes the horrible pains called withdrawal symptoms when the alcoholic stops drinking after building up a high level of alcohol in his or her system;
- does cause confusion and occasional memory loss or temporary amnesia;
- causes a preoccupation with getting adequate supplies of beverage alcohol so that it destroys the person's sense of priorities, distorts the alcoholic's awareness of time, and upsets his or her economic stability;
- moves the drinker from consciousness to various states of semiconsciousness to unconsciousness;
- brings a marked personality change in the drinker;
- brings about a morality change—one in which the drinker will lie, cheat, and steal to maintain the addiction to alcohol while trying to maintain his or her social relationships.

The American Medical Society officially recognized the disease definition of chemical dependency in relationship to alcohol and other sedatives in 1956. They declared that the alcoholic person has an incurable disease unless the alcohol intake ceases. Greater consumption will drive the alcoholic toward a worse case of alcoholism and then toward death. While the alcoholic may have more personal power to withstand the first drink of any series, he or she does develop a craving and has a more than the normal temptation to drink.

Alcoholism is drawing much attention today because of the massive damage it does to the health of the drinker, the lower productivity shown on the job, and the great damage he or she may do while operating an industrial machine or a motor vehicle. Today across the world governments are tightening the loopholes in their laws to be able to punish people who drink and injure others—especially in the flying of airplanes, the piloting of ocean vessels, and the operation of cars, trucks, and trains. New laws with harsh penalties are being added to the books, and in some places the volume of beverage alcohol sales is dropping.

There is a great uproar heard from those who manufacture, distribute, and sell alcoholic beverages against the stricter drunk driving laws. But even they are beginning to work, however grudgingly, in the direction of trying to create a sober driving public. They are aware of laws in many other countries where a drunken driver may forfeit not only his license, but also his automobile. A drunken driver may be heavily fined for a first offense and do time in jail; this depends on whether he has injured or killed someone or not. In more primitive countries, a drunken driver may also lose his hand.

By comparison, the American justice system has been very gentle. Now, even those who wish to continue their profit making by selling alcoholic beverages are coming to understand they must join in the struggle for responsible use of their products.

But the number of persons damaged and injured in these ways by alcoholics is actually very small when compared to the damage done to the tender personalities of their families, especially the children. The results of problem drinking and alcoholism on the family are coming to be regarded by some people as the single most contributing factor in the widespread activity of child and spouse abuse in the United States. This is especially true when you consider the large numbers of children growing to adulthood who are emotionally handicapped due to their relationships with alcoholics. Alcoholic families produce more codependent persons than any other source in the United States.

Helpful Information from the Addiction Studies[4]

Researchers are uniformly agreed that codependence is an addiction. Unlike the substance addictions (alcohol, cigarettes, food, drugs), the event addictions (gambling, workaholism, spree shopping, spending), or the abuse addictions (sexual, physical beatings), *codependence is a relationship addiction. Just as the alcoholic is addicted to the alcohol, the codependent is attached to the addict.* But addictions are more alike one another than they are unlike one another. Actually, all addictions have many things in common. Several of those common characteristics show up in codependency studies. Some of the more prominent are as follows.

First, addictions are attractive to people because they provide benefits that are worthwhile from the addict's point of view. In spite of what they look like to outsiders, addictions have the ability to interrupt pain or a bad mood while they give comfort to the addict and lift his spirits. This is the distorted way of thinking often referred to as *addictive logic.* The addiction produces a significant mood change usually in three areas. Whenever the addict has a sense of being out of control, taking a drink or getting into his addictive practice gives him the illusion that he is now in control. Whenever he feels uncomfortable, his addiction restores him to comfort. Whenever he judges himself to be imperfect, especially more imperfect than usual, when he reactivates his addictive process, he has the illusion of perfection. The seductive part of addiction is in its promise to give the addict at least the feeling of being better off than he was.

In the second place, addicts tend to be persons who prefer extreme positions in thought and action. When an addict is recovering from the extreme use of one addiction, she may swing radically to the extreme use of another addiction. Or, she may switch to radical sobriety. People who prefer extremes usually do not prefer to do anything in moderation.[5]

Third, an addiction, once acquired, makes a permanent change in the individual. If you become addicted, you may find a way to escape the substance, event, abuse, or relationship addiction, but it always lies beneath the surface of your personality ready to be reactivated at any time. You may recover from addiction, but you cannot be cured.

Next, an addiction is a progressive process; it begins mildly enough with the addict believing she will never become "hooked." It moves through the three basic stages of internal change, external or life-style change, and terminal or breakdown stage. As time passes, the addict is drawn deeper into the addiction, to stages of more complete isolation, or in the case of substance abuse, to stages of disability or death.

Addiction is, in the fifth place, a belief that things are never going to get better for you in the world of reality. Because the path of addiction avoids reality and helps you to bypass the unpleasant side of reality, it launches you forward into life with the idea that you are doomed in the real world. Addictive logic teaches that you had better live in a fantasy world. Addiction sinks the addict into a negative life-style. Whenever reality crowds normal persons, they reach for their resources: family, friends, religious faith, and deep within themselves. Harsh as it may be, the normal person with support faces the music. The addict, on the other hand, avoids the harshness of reality. Retreating into addiction usually makes things far worse in reality; but, within the addictive system and according to addictive logic (within the fantasy world where the addict lives), the addict rests secure as if he were in control, completely comfortable, and perfect.

Finally, shame becomes an ever-present feeling for the addict. Guilt is strongly denied, and blame is loudly placed on some other person or set of circumstances. "If I had a better break." "If you had just called me in time." Sometimes the excuses are not rational at all, but they fit well into addictive logic. However, the sense of shame builds over time. The addiction eventually brings about outward signs of loss of control: you lose emotional control and "lose your cool"; you lose mental control and forget or hallucinate; and finally in the last stages, you lose physical control. This cannot be hidden forever. Your friends and family cannot give you a perfect enough cover to protect you from the outside world. Your drinking, your multiple sexual affairs, your excessive spending beyond your income will finally show up. You may begin with some form of mild embarrassment, later you may feel badly about the way you forget things. But the creeping feeling of shame arises unmistakably with great energy as your control centers are lost to you. This is often so upsetting to alcoholics that they withdraw more intensely from everyone in shame. They cannot do what they were formerly able to do, and they do the things they would not previously have done. Shame becomes a constant companion, and they experience a pain much more terrible than the pain the addiction was originally begun to erase.

A Person's Vulnerability to Addiction

The personality pattern of addicts of all kinds has formed a clear and recognizable profile. They do not have, and seemingly do not know how to have, healthy relationships. They have no skills of negotiation or conflict management abilities. They do not trust people. They isolate themselves and attempt to solve their problems themselves. They do not seem to be able to initiate or sustain intimacy even with spouse or children. Their relationships within the family are formal, rather stilted, and follow tradition. They exist together under the same roof.

The people most vulnerable to addiction, then, are people who grow into adults with such personality profiles. Those who have not learned to trust other people are especially vulnerable. Children deserve, among other things in life, a context of affection in which to grow and develop. They need trustworthy parenting persons. Individuals who have not learned to trust and who consequently are afraid to tell the truth, who experienced untrustworthy or inconsistent parenting in such tasks as rule setting and discipline—these people are especially vulnerable to addiction.

People who do not know how to have healthy relationships are also vulnerable. This cuts them off from trustworthy sources of comfort and support in the face of a real world with its problems and harshness as well as its opportunities. Children are handicapped when they grow through childhood without developing warm "chumships" and friendships, when they have not been supported by caring and knowledgeable adults through the tumultuous and stressful times of puberty and the teen years, and when they have not learned to relate with self-assurance to same sex and opposite sex peers, to adults in authority, and to the society in which they live. They are unprepared to face reality with courage and support.

If they grow through early life and do not have their minds exercised at least to the level of dealing with some of the difficulties they will face, if they are not challenged away from the practice of childhood fantasy as a method of dealing with troubles, if they remain addicted to magical thinking to manage the things they fear or do not understand, then they will be vulnerable to addiction.

A Suggestion About Prevention and Recovery

Addiction is a seductive process. Information about addiction as a way to behave should be introduced early in the learning process of children. The counselors and researchers who work in this field suggest several strategies for presenting this information to children. A most fruitful approach in terms of belief systems is the strategy based on the idea of hope.

You hope no one you care about will begin to be addicted. You hope no part of a loved one's personality will be taken captive by addiction. Actually, any part of a person's life can be targets to be captured by the addictive process: the mind, emotions, body, spirit, or will. Yet hope remains in those parts of your person not captured by addiction.

When people are serious about preparing to do battle with the temptations offered by a variety of addictions, they will spend time strengthening those parts of themselves that fight against addiction. They develop the best possible relationship skills, nurture wholesome relationships, and sustain intimacy with those they trust. They stay in touch with them, pledge never to withdraw from them, and make a pact to be open with them—giving them permission to inquire, to look in on you from time to time.

This support system is especially important in times of crisis—at the times of the death of a loved one, or any significant loss; when you have an illness; lose a job; fail in something important to you. Closeness and intimate friendships are good insurance policies against temptations to addiction.

A strong spiritual life is an especially vital strength. What you are before God in the inner recesses of your soul may at times be the only cord of strength left to you to resist the temptation of the unreality of addiction.

Once addicted, however, this strategy of hope is even more useful. As you grapple with a place to begin the task of escape from addiction, or as you seek to stand by friends who are struggling to recover, nurture in their minds the truth that the addiction has not conquered all of their heart, mind, and soul. The parts of them not addicted can, will, must, rise up and drive the invading addiction out. The first step in recovery for many addicts is to accept the concept that part of their inner selves is not addicted. It is with the nonaddicted parts that the addicts themselves, the counselors, friends, and Almighty God begin to work toward recovery.

The Development of Self-Help Groups

One major development in the field of addiction is Alcoholics Anonymous. Begun in 1935 in the United States, AA was a self-help group of alcoholics who, when they were sober, were bound together with the pledge to stay sober and to help any other alcoholic who wished to join them to stay sober. By the late 1980s, more than twenty-five thousand Alcoholics Anonymous groups existed in the United States, and they have spread across the world among industrialized nations.

Their success rate in helping alcoholics who want to remain sober to do so is remarkable. And the principles they follow include both a spiritual dimension and an interpersonal dimension. Their plan for the recovery of alcoholics has changed through the years, but mostly it has intensified rather than changed. Strict adherence to their suggested program of recovery includes following a twelve-step plan in order and to the letter, to have a sponsor who is a recovering alcoholic, and to attend AA meetings once a day for at least ninety days—preferably once a day for the first 365 days, and then three days per week as long as you are able. The twelve steps are as follows:

1. We admitted we were powerless over alcohol—that our lives had become unmanageable.

2. Came to believe that a Power greater than ourselves could restore us to sanity.

3. Made a decision to turn our will and our lives over to the care of God as we understood Him.

4. Made a searching and fearless moral inventory of ourselves.

5. Admitted to God, to ourselves, and to another human being the exact nature of our wrongs.

6. Were entirely ready to have God remove all these defects of character.

7. Humbly asked him to remove all our shortcomings.

8. Made a list of all persons we had harmed, and became willing to make amends to them all.

9. Made direct amends to such people whenever possible, except when to do so would injure them or others.

10. Continued to take personal inventory and when we were wrong promptly admitted it.

11. Sought through prayer and meditation to improve our conscious contact with God as we understood him, praying only for knowledge of His will for us and the power to carry that out.

12. Having had a spiritual awakening as the result of these steps, we tried to carry this message to alcoholics and to practice these principles in all our affairs.[6]

Members of Alcoholics Anonymous come from all walks of life, and at first they formed a fraternity, an organization, focused almost entirely on the needs of the alcoholic member. They established a recovery plan on a broad general principle of spirituality that has brought remarkable success to millions of alcoholics. It is to this principle of spirituality that Christians need to give special attention. Whatever medical or psychological means are developed to help, the massive attention given by members of the Alcoholics Anonymous groups across the years to the need for spirituality as a basis for cure is an important reaffirmation from the very pit of illness and sin itself to those of us who carry the banner of Jesus Christ. Spirituality is not an automatic answer, of course, and a generalized spirituality without process, content, or direction will not suffice. But placed in its proper frame of reference and made available to addicts, the spirituality approach may well afford Christians a new window of opportunity to assist alcoholics and codependents.

In the beginning of the organization of Alcoholics Anonymous, however, you received little or no attention if you were a member of the alcoholic's family. By the mid 1940s, a group of spouses (mostly wives) of alcoholics began their own group and called it Al Anon. These people met together weekly, or more often if necessary, to give each other moral support and to swap ideas about how to survive with an alcoholic spouse.

In the late 1950s and early 1960s, the medical and counseling professions began to take a careful interest in the importance of the families of alcoholics. Family medicine, especially in psychiatry, began to grow in influence. Counselors of several professions had begun to move toward the care of individuals in what they often called group therapy, sometimes designed as artificial families, and here and there actual families were seen together by the counselors.

Alcoholics rarely presented themselves for therapy, although their families were often seeking help for themselves. Al Anon was very successful and has fostered Ala-teen and a host of other twelve-step support groups for family members of alcoholics and other codependents. These meetings are held in many places, but almost always bring about the same results: help and hope for the participants. The persons involved discover they are no longer alone, no longer need to feel themselves weird, unique, or the only people in God's universe suffering like themselves. The twelve-step self-help movements have been praised by every helping professional group with enough forthrightness to investigate before making a judgment. These self-help groups were often rejected for superficial reasons, yet they often offered the only place in town where people could receive open and unconditional acceptance.

Other Approaches to Addiction and Addicts' Families

The Emmanuel Movement[7] was a unique combination of religion and psychiatry. It attempted to treat a variety of other diseases well known to the medical community, but its full energies were focused on attempting to find a method to cure alcoholics. This unusual combination of medical and church resources were combined during the period between 1906 and 1940 in Boston at the Emmanuel Episcopal Church where two ministers, Elwood Worcester and Samuel McComb, provided the major input from the religious community.

Its treatment process included a series of group meetings called classes but conducted in the fashion of therapy. Individual conferences with alcoholics were held daily at the clinics, and a pattern of attention similar to that of social work was conducted by visitors to the homes of the patients. It flourished in the United States and was imitated overseas. The treatment was administered in three stages, the first being an open confessional, the second being "prayer and godly counsel," and the third stage included the use of some medical techniques such as hypnosis and hypnotic suggestion.

The uniqueness of this program is evident, but it ended with the death of its founders. The use of intensive group work combined with individual work was innovative. The Emmanuel Movement goal of "reconstruction of the inner life so the alcoholic could remain abstinent" was an important theme in recovery programs in the 1980s.

Other groups have also been active in the field of providing help for alcoholic addicts and their families. Although alcoholics perceived the church as a good place for ordinary people to have their spiritual needs met, most of them stayed away primarily because of their deep feelings of guilt and shame. The evangelical churches continually preached against the use of alcohol as sin and alcoholics as sinners. Addicts perceived themselves as misunderstood and rejected. Church attempts in the areas of rescue mission work were thought to be nice when alcoholics were down-and-out; and when they were really out of money, friends, and luck, listening to a sermon was a small price to pay for a bath, a good meal, and a warm, clean bed. There have been some remarkable incidents of alcoholics finding religious faith, of their being converted in an alcoholic mission chapel. Many have recovered, rebuilt fortunes, and given of their means to sustain the mission movement. Mostly, however, the mission movement has been a stopgap activity, filling in the blanks between binges of alcoholics.

Some churches sponsored chapters of Alcoholics Anonymous, sometimes calling them Parish Fellowships. These seem to have enjoyed successes equal to those reported by the regular Alcoholics Anonymous groups.

Through the years, the Salvation Army has included an intentional ministry to alcoholics as part of its rescue mission ministry. They have combined the unique strategy of the Emmanuel Movement, that of having regularly scheduled group meetings and individual counseling available, with a standard mission center worship routine. They have also added a residential facility for alcoholics to recover. Salvation Army social services are also supportive of families of alcoholics cared for in its shelters. The Salvation Army centers for alcoholics seem to have begun shortly before the close of the Emmanuel centers.

A more popular counseling strategy also demonstrated direct interest in alcoholics and members of their families. In his popular book, first issued in 1964, called *Games People Play,* Eric Berne wrote a game called "Alcoholic." In the game, the family members and close associates of alcoholics were described as people who were locked into a series of transactions with the heavy drinker. He listed roles they played in the game. The *alcoholic* is the leading role; he or she is "it." The *persecutor* is a game player whose condemnation and nagging drove and/or keeps driving the alcoholic to drink. Sometimes, a spouse or a parent plays the part of a persecutor. A third player is the *rescuer*, often an upright (sober) friend such as a doctor or member of the clergy and sometimes the spouse or parent, who tries to rescue the alcoholic from the drinking habit. After a period of sobriety, the rescuer usually congratulates the alcoholic on his or her success, and the next day the alcoholic is dead drunk—again.

And the game goes on.

Another major player is the *patsy*, the one who most often takes it on the chin for the alcoholic's excesses. Often a marriage partner, a parent, another family member, or a good friend who owes the alcoholic a big favor loans money to the alcoholic and provides a maximum amount of protection for him. All the while, the patsy convinces herself the alcoholic will reform and use the money for debts and to get on his feet again.

Two other roles are identified in the game. First is the *agitator*, the person who often provides free drinks for the alcoholic "just to be sociable" even when not asked to do so and usually just to uphold his "good-guy" status. The agitator is a troublesome role in the game. The second and most curious other person in the game, the *connection*, is the person who is either a drinking buddy who keeps the alcoholic from killing himself or the bartender who knows when to start serving coffee and to call a cab to take the customer home.

Also in this same book, Berne spoke briefly of the alternate game of "Dry Alcoholic," a game for addicts who do not drink beverage alcohol, but who are addicted to substances or processes other than alcohol. The way the game is played is the same, Berne says, and the same kinds of people are required for the game. The only difference is that each episode of the game may be played faster.

This careful description by Eric Berne of the game of wet or dry "Alcoholic," which he calls a life script or a pattern lived by great numbers of people, is but a single example of the way a variety of counselors had begun to think about alcoholics and the supportive cast around them.

At the same time, marriage and family counselors were developing new concepts. Basically, they grouped a large list of family problems under the heading of *dysfunctional* families. They were discovering that the ways families lived caused difficulties for their children as they were growing up. Adolescents were still seen as being delinquent, but there came a period when parents were discovered as playing a strongly contributing role in that delinquency—in some cases even playing a major part in it.

Counselors also began to understand how young adults who grew up in dysfunctional families were recreating the problems of their parents. Often they were actually making new families more creatively dysfunctional than their parents' families. Secular departments of marriage and family studies began to study the statistics related to divorce. While some people spent all their time complaining about the terrible divorce rate, and it was and is terrible, they missed the root causes of so much of the divorcing.

Christian marriage and family teachers struggled to catch the attention of the denominations and churches to give proper attention to the family and its troubles. In the late 1950s and the early 1960s, the powerful forces operating inside families that destroyed the promised "paradise" spoken of in the Bible began to receive additional attention by ministers and lay leaders in the churches.

Helpful Information from Addiction Research[8]

Addiction researchers have added helpful information. They have clarified the process by which addiction occurs, a process that seems to operate no matter what the focus of addiction. Compulsive shopping as a habit pattern, or addiction, gets into a person's system by just the same set of steps as problem drinking, workaholism, child abuse, cocaine abuse, overeating, or compulsive gambling.

Addiction begins innocently enough as an attempt to "feel good." This move toward good feeling is usually in response to some unpleasant feelings encountered in some setting or in some relationship likely to be repeated often in the person's life. It begins as an innocent avoidance maneuver. Whatever is attempted, say overeating for example, gives a person the warm and pleasant feelings associated with food, allowing the person to forget about the harsh reality of a bad grade at school or a scolding from a parent. If the unpleasant feelings are successfully avoided, then food will be used as an escape again, until in a short time overeating becomes the method of choice to avoid any kind of bad feelings. Overeating puts distance between the addict and others both emotionally—you don't face the feelings really stimulated in the relationship—and physically—you become fat and put more actual distance between yourself and others.

Until now, the addiction is in an introductory phase. Soon the addict begins to tell himself, I should not be doing all this. It's not good for my health. And he begins an inner dialogue between his free self and the addicted self. Just so long as the addiction gives him a way to control pain, to comfort himself, and to see himself as more "perfect," the addicted self gains in power over the free self. The addictive self becomes a master of illusion. Almost by magical means (by the vehicle of the daydream) the person avoids pain through the addictive patterns and substance. Never mind what is really happening, that the other people involved see him as moving away, as moody, as withdrawn. He doesn't know that. He is instructed by the addictive self not to care. Addictive logic begins to develop: he really is in control, he really should not have to hurt, he really is OK, so don't sweat any unhappy relationship; let's go get a burger, or a pizza, and a coke.

When this internal change is near, stage 1 is nearing completion. Stage 2 kicks in with the internal change taking over the outward actions. What is in his mind now works its way into standard practice. The addictive self is in the driver's seat. He sets up his rituals to maintain his addiction. He hides candy in places he may be alone. He has high-calorie between-meal snacks available throughout the day. But he eats with friends and eats a normal or even a diet meal to foster the illusion he is trying to lose weight and join the slim set. But he never gives up his addiction. The hallmark of stage two addiction is the spiritual emptiness a person feels. He has no connection between himself and God with this addiction, except when his addicted mind is in control begging God by some miracle to allow him to be thin, yet still eat to his heart's content. The hidden goal of addiction is seen here. The hidden goal of addiction from outset to end is spiritual death.[9]

The third and final stage of addiction is the stage of life breakdown. The addictive self is in total control, but there is a lack of genuine pleasure in life. Terrifyingly, the addict either establishes total control or a spiral of increased abuse, neglect, and shame behavior rules the day. Those accustomed to the more productive forms of addiction may become more exceptionally workaholic; they will start two new businesses, and if they have enough emotional energy to do those without destroying themselves, they start enough businesses until they self-destruct. Or, they will withdraw from the only things that formerly gave meaning to them. For example, they will leave their marriage partners of twenty-five years or more with the vague statements, "I don't love you any more," "Life was passing me by, and I just had to get out," or "I don't know what is bothering me; I don't want a divorce, I just want whatever is going on to stop." Such statements are primary evidence that the covert addictions, and especially codependence as addiction, has the person in its stern grip.

According to the addiction researchers, cure for addiction includes a three-point process. First, addicts must accept the reality of the dual personality struggle within. Nakken says this creates a door that opens inward, allowing them to begin to establish an honest relationship. From that point forward, the commitment to honesty must be the new addiction. Without it, at least seven more addictions will rush in to replace the one that has been banished from the inner house. (See Matt. 12:43-45.) Second, they must get in touch with their true spirituality. Trust in God and the discovery of hope for recovery is essential for the often long and arduous tasks ahead. Intimacy is such a new phenomenon that it should not be rushed. It must not be artificially administered or stimulated. It must be given birth in the most wholesome ways.

Confession and an experience of acceptance/grace is paramount. Steadfastness on the part of a friend or friends and, where present, steadfastness and genuine unconditional love from family are vital. Positive rituals of connectedness to replace the addictive rituals of separateness are so important they may also be essential.

Evidence of Codependent Personalities in Other Places

Alcoholic families are not the only families producing codependent offspring. Since the clarification of the codependent personality, it has been discovered that children of alcoholic families develop in "unhappy" patterns almost identical in outcome to children reared in dysfunctional families. Strangely enough, children of families with parents afflicted with any kind of addiction produced children with similar dysfunctional life-styles. The personality pattern first discovered by the alcoholic researchers and then labeled by those who worked with their family members began showing up in all kinds of dysfunctional and abusive families. Thus the pool from which lists of symptoms for codependents could be selected grew by leaps and bounds.

But the original breakthrough of understanding and description of the process we have come to call codependence came to a group of counselors who were working with a massive group of families suffering because one or more of their members was addicted to alcohol. They are the people who are responsible for discovering, or at least publicizing, the discovery we are coming to know as codependence.

The Emergence of the Word Codependence

Sometime in the 1980s the terms *codependency* and *codependent* seemed to emerge simultaneously in the clinical case conferences, the public presentations, and the pamphlet literature of different centers where alcoholics were in treatment. Melody Beattie, the author of a *New York Times* best seller, *Co-dependent No More,* surmises that they were probably first used in Minnesota, still the "heartland of chemical dependency treatment and

Twelve Step programs for compulsive disorders."[10]

Since 1989 the term *codependency* has emerged as the single most-used term to define the style of life of the family members and other people whose lives have become tangled up with and deeply influenced by alcoholics. Books about codependence have been flooding the marketplace in the United States since the middle of the 1980s. The book that launched the term *codependency* in print for the general public was the Health Communications, Inc. book *Co-Dependency: An Emerging Issue.* This book was a reprinting of a collection of a dozen articles from two journals, *Focus on the Family* and *Chemical Dependency.* Since then, nearly three dozen popular books about codependency have appeared. Nearly one hundred such books were scheduled to be available to the public by the end of 1989. Some of the better ones, as judged by this author, are listed in the bibliography at the end of this book.

What Then Is Codependence?

Codependence has been described in this book as an addiction: something to which you are compelled, something that once you begin it, you do not have the power to stop. You are locked in by an invisible plan in your personality or life-style that was planted there a long time ago. You may stop it, but you will have to have a great deal of help.

Mary's story illustrates the addict in John's behavior, and really highlights one kind of codependence in Mary. From Mary and those like her we learn that the codependent

- is an addict, a special kind of addict, but an addict none the less;
- is addicted to a life-style of compulsive helping, rescuing of others whom she loves;
- has a very low estimate of personal self-worth and must, like Mary, take care of everything to be valuable;
- believes everything that goes wrong is her fault;
- will cover for, clean up for, lie, and protect the addict(s) she loves;
- controls feelings, especially negative ones;

- believes she deserves nothing good, not even the outward signs of love from her own children, although she desperately wants it;
- will work as long as it takes, sacrifice as much as there is, will bear as much scorn or pity as necessary to get the job done;
- will fight and argue if and when she thinks she may gain something, but otherwise usually avoids conflict;
- is driven by shame, the feeling side of the "I'm bad" judgments, and also steered by guilt, the feeling side of the "I ought to" judgments;
- will wait as long as necessary to achieve goals if her wish fantasy (that things really will get better by and by) is still alive;
- constantly worries and has real physical diseases like migraine headaches, ulcers, and other stress problems;
- beneath all the obvious pain, she is striving to keep control and to gain more control (Mary contained her own feelings, was pleased her girls did what she wanted without her asking—silent control—and kept others at a distance);
- never uses energy or money for herself; lives like a martyr, like Mary with no winter clothing;
- did not feel love and approval from her parents, and rarely gives sufficient supplies of affection and unconditional love to her own children;
- pretends circumstances are not as bad as they are, and really believes things will be better; really has a partial illusion that magical things will happen to heal her situation;
- tolerates spouse's abuse and cherishes each little tidbit of kindness and affection he gives her; hopes for the love the husband has really never learned to give (John is a flatterer, not a lover; he was not programmed for the long haul, only for short-term relationships, only long enough to make a sale);
- avoids talking with anyone about her feelings and inner thoughts; she has no intimate friends;
- has no romance, no goals, no joys, just work and avoidance of anything else to bring shame on herself and her family; she is existing, not living;

•has begun to feel hopeless.

Chapter Summary

Early in the history of codependence, the definition of the word was fairly simple and clear. Codependence was understood to be the bond that ties a person to an addict, and mostly an alcoholic addict. This person said to have codependence was then called a codependent person. Codependence actually was seen to bring about a style of relationship between persons in which some broadly defined rules were active. The features of this relationship were essentially as follows: The addicts (alcoholics) had the right to drink and be drunk or not to drink and be sober whenever they chose. They had the right to be responsible, irresponsible, loving or hateful, social or antisocial, tender or abusive, law abiding or lawless whenever they chose.

The codependents accepted the condition of abuse from the addicts. They behaved as if it were their duty to clean up the messes made by the addicts, to make endless excuses for the addicts to members of their families, employers and fellow employees, neighbors, and friends. They understood that they might have to care for the household without assistance from their mates—including the rearing of the children. They often also had to go to work to see that the bills got paid and food was on the table. They may even have had to lie for their addicts to save their jobs and tell half-truths to everyone in an attempt to preserve friendships or save face for the family.

The codependents may have had to take over all job responsibilities of family life, even those formerly chosen by their spouses as their own contribution to the marriage: caring for the car, doing the yard work, and repairing and keeping up the house. They may have had to make all major decisions without consultation with their spouses; and they did all of this just so their mates could be free to follow their addiction.

If the woman were the addict and her husband were the codependent, then the male codependent often found himself providing or paying for all the custodial care for the children, planning all the meals without assistance from his wife while she was drinking, caring for her previously selected chores, and in general, doing everything without open and supportive consultation with his wife. All of this in addition to making excuses, telling half-truths, and boldly lying about her behavior in an effort to cover up or hide the truth of the addiction.

Other family members participated in the drama of codependence. People in love relationships with addicts fell into obvious codependent relationships with them. Parents of addicts, especially alcoholics, continually provided havens of rest for addicts. Often they set them on their feet again, giving them sums of money to "start all over again." Occasionally, the cure worked. In a greater number of cases, the "rescued one" returned to the bottle and fell deeper into the addiction.

In poorer families where enough money was not available to set the addict on his feet, giving him a bed and some food, then giving him a little of mother's love, care, laundry, spending money, and sometimes special pleading with an employer to give him a job were gratefully received by the addict. Rarely did the cycle of addiction break here. The addict spent a period of months away from the bottle, staying sober only until things seemed better. Then just as things were looking up, the addict began to drink again, and the strong codependent community around him was challenged to come to his defense again, cover for him, clean up his messes, and try harder the next time to get him sober and keep him sober.

Little attention in this early period was paid to the children of an addict/codependent relationship. Most people extended their pity to the youngsters. Some well-meaning folk extended a helping hand, provided resources to assist the children in the areas of education and development of their talents. But there was an unusual amount of sentimentality, which reinforced the feelings of inferiority in the children.

The church, and Christians in general, spoke out to this obvious problem in society. Some churches spoke out forthrightly against alcoholic drink and the human drunkenness it produced, calling it sin. Its preachers and laypeople exhorted alcoholics to repent of this evil habit and to come to faith in Christ, who would forgive past sins and bring them to new birth and new life in the community of Christianity. Mission centers and inner-city preaching stations were established in our major cities. Because there had been some significant examples of such conversions in recent public evangelical memory, there was some reason to hope this method would succeed.

Some alcoholics responded to this approach. They received Christ by faith and were spiritually cleansed of their alcoholic addiction. The great masses of alcoholics, however, were not reached by this method. Many were actually driven from the church by it; but fortunately there were other persons standing by to care for them.

Alcoholics Anonymous, started in 1935, began to spread throughout the United States and in other countries. Al-Anon and other self-help groups began to meet some of the needs of family members and friends of addicts.

The so-called twelve-step program was further refined and developed into a methodology that met people at the level of their deepest needs and was within the range of their own understanding. It majored on the responsibility of the addict for his own condition and provided for the appropriate external support of sponsors and fellow addicts. Its major feature was its open advertisement as a "spiritual" method of treatment. While the treatment was much like open worship to the unknown God that Paul found in Athens, at least it was not completely secular, not drug related, not magic, not humanistic. It is spiritual in nature. This is a good place for Christians to begin dialogue with themselves and with alcoholics and other addicts.

The stage was set for further observation of codependents. It was time to listen intently to what they had to say, to watch carefully what they were doing, and to see if additional insights could be gained about how their particular patterns of life developed. Such information just possibly could help professional persons to learn how to work at the tasks of prevention and cure.

The word *cure* seems to have been the hope of the original researchers. Currently, the concept of continuous and never-ending "recovery" has replaced the concept of "cure" with regards to codependents as well as alcoholics.

Of special note is the further refinement of the definition of the personality style of the person called a codependent. Information from the many counseling disciplines continued to pour into the public dialogue through books and periodicals. The careful study of dysfunctional families verified the presence of addictive/codependent marriage partners. Family studies verified the kinds and styles of dysfunctional family patterns created by these mating patterns. Children reared in these homes were discovered to possess similar characteristics, which presented them to the real world with a variety of emotional and social handicaps as well as crippled interactional patterns and skills.

Chapter 2 will outline some of the symptoms and patterns discovered that enriched the ongoing history of the concept of codependence and will conclude with a more broadened definition.

Notes

1. Gerald G. May, *Addiction and Grace* (San Francisco: Harper and Row, 1988). The relationship of codependency and addiction is one of the main themes of this excellent book.

2. The following information follows the description in the *Diagnostic and Statistical Manual of Mental Disorders*, 3d ed., rev. (Washington, D.C.: American Psychiatric Association, 1987), 127-35, 173-75. Another interesting classification and important research document is E. M. Jelinek's work *The Disease Concept of Alcoholism* (New Haven, Conn.: Hillhouse, 1960) in which he proposed a carefully outlined five-type theory of alcohol dependence based on the physical disease concept. It is still considered a standard work in the field. See also, Donald M. Gallant, *Alcoholism: A Guide to Diagnosis, Intervention, and Treatment* (New York: W. W. Norton & Company, 1987), 11. Gallant insists a person is an alcoholic if sufficient alcohol is consumed by a person to interfere to the level requiring treatment in one of the following five areas of a person's life: "job or studies, relationships within the home, social relationships, legal problems, or medical complications."

3. *Diagnostic and Statistical Manual of Mental Disorders*, 173-75.

4. Craig Nakken, *The Addictive Personality: Understanding Compulsion in Our Lives*

(San Francisco: Harper/Hazelton, 1988), 1-63; Arnold Ludwig, *Understanding the Alcoholic's Mind: The Nature of Craving and How to Control It* (New York: Oxford Press, 1988), 69-90; Gallant, 86 *ff.*

5. See the thesis of E. Hoffer's book *The True Believer* (New York: Harper, 1951).

6. *Alcoholics Anonymous*, 3d ed. (New York: Alcoholics Anonymous World Services, 1976), 59-60.

7. All material written here about the Emmanuel Movement is found in Howard J. Clinebell, Jr., *Understanding the Alcoholic* (Nashville: Abingdon Press, 1956), 94-109.

8. The outline and major material for this section has been borrowed with gratitude from Craig Nakken, *The Addictive Personality*, 19-62.

9. Ibid., 54.

10. Melody Beattie, *Codependent No More: How to Stop Controlling Others and Start Caring for Yourself* (New York: Harper and Row, 1987), 29.

2

What Do Codependents Really Look Like?

Family Patterns Creating Codependence

New information has been added almost every six months for the past several years to enlarge the picture of codependence. In addition to the earliest snapshots taken of codependence among family members of alcoholics, at least four new angles of vision have given us important new information.

First, *families that operate with a rigid set of rules consistently produce codependent members, both adults and children.* Many if not most of the rules apply to families with alcoholic members. But they really apply to any family. Actually, when you read about them, you may discover that your own family operated by some of these same rules. Some of you will say, "That's exactly how my family operated," or at least, "That's exactly how my family operated whenever Uncle Jake was concerned." Families with specifically defined rules seem to produce codependent persons. (These rules will be listed and described later in the chapter.)

A second clue to the origin of codependent persons relates to a pattern of roles some families seem to assign to themselves. *Families who live in a system with carefully designed roles that are fulfilled by each member produce codependent persons.* A careful system of roles was discovered to exist in families that have and produce codependent persons. These roles are lived out so well it is just as if a playwright had written out a script for them to follow. Almost always "in character," persons with assigned roles usually follow their parts quite well. If a person who was supposed to play an assigned role was absent, moved away, or died, somebody else in the family usually became a stand-in for him or her. Families with fairly rigid role assignments of a particular kind usually produce codependent persons.

Third, the study of adults who had grown up in homes with an addicted parent revealed a standard kind of personality structure that is clearly seen as codependent. Usually called Adult Children of Alcoholics (ACOAs, or more recently ACAs), these persons have received very prominent coverage in popular literature and professional journals. They can be identified because they have great pain in personal and interpersonal relationships, can be easily diagnosed, are usually well employed, can pay standard fees for treatment, and so receive some of the better-funded responses to medical problems.

Because of the great number of substance abusers in the United States, their children make up a sizable segment of the population. This is a large group, one in which you may discover yourself to be a part. *Persons who grow up in homes with one or more addicted parents develop a personality style of codependence. When they are adults, they now are referred to as being Adult Children of an Alcoholic.* A snapshot of the ACA personality style is remarkable because when several of the characteristics are combined to form a random but very clear pattern, the person stands out and can be recognized as an ACA by friends and close acquaintances. ACAs consistently marry each other and produce codependent children.

A fourth and more diverse group of codependent characteristics has been discovered in relationship to a wide variety of addictions. *Some people develop a single cluster of major personality characteristics that causes them to function as codependent persons in part of their lives. They may or may not also develop one of the so-called minor addictions as part of that cluster.* The addictions may be so slight as to appear harmless on the surface or else are so obvious that others do not even relate to them as addictions. Most of these addictions are listed and described in ways related to the kinds of codependent partnerships these so-called single-cluster codependents and minor addicts tend to seek.

There is a fifth and final group that is worthy of mention. *This special group of codependents is made up of people whose vocations or professional lives are spent in the task of "rescuing" those in need.* They are the paid codependents of our society whose vocations or professional lives are "masking" their membership in the codependent family. Doctors, ministers, secretaries, EMS workers, and nurses are the most obvious examples. These are plainly examples of the codependence pattern put to useful service of humanity's need for care.

Other combinations of the characteristics of codependents are possible. *There are persons who are both addicts and codependents at the same time.* They are addicts because they have become addicted to alcohol or one of the more recognizable forms of addiction, and they also exhibit one or more of the major characteristics of the codependent personality style. They are either codependent addicts or addicted codependents. In addition, there are those who are *multiple addicts.* They are hooked on more than one of the addictive substances or processes we all recognize as addictions. And then there are situations where *families seem to produce codependent offspring because the parents are themselves codependent, and there have been no alcoholics or other substance abuse addicts in the family for two or three generations.* Of course, life-styles are frequently reproduced for generations after the major addiction, but we must not neglect the subtle addictions often in the cleanest appearing environments. And there are other combinations in as many clever styles as creative evil has been able to produce in the lives of persons.

Before describing the individual sources of codependent persons, it might be well to say a word about the kind of home environments that would allow such life-styles to develop. Surely, you say, they would not be allowed to develop in homes where both parents were trying to do the right kind of job rearing a family, where the adults would be on guard not to allow such a crippling pattern or set of patterns to be implanted in the personalities of their children. Unfortunately, the transmission is mostly unconscious. The characteristics are passed on almost as silently as the color of eyes and the texture of the hair. Once the patterns are in a family, they are there for a long time.

Codependents have been trained in a wide variety of environments. As individuals, they may have lived all their lives in one home environment. Or, they may have experienced more than one kind of family background. If they spent much time in the home of a relative, such as the home of grandparents, they may have a variety of experiences. If they spent long periods of time in the home(s) of codependent sitters, they may well have learned the codependent patterns in those relationships. They also may come from a traditional family, a blended family, a single-parent family, or from a foster home. They may have come from homes rich or poor, religious or nonreligious. They may not have had a regular home experience at all. Codependence is just as easily taught and learned in public as well as in private institutional environments.

In order to have the widest possible understanding of codependence, it is good to understand that no single kind of place or environment produces codependent personality styles. You must look into the different kinds of training camps from which they came for basic orientation. In that way, you can begin to see the constant characteristics in the different places. Then the picture of a codependent will emerge.

But something else will happen for you. You will begin to see the enormity of the task facing the counseling professionals. How do they, or anyone for that matter, get a hold on the actual characteristics of this codependence thing? How can we assist codependents who want to recover to do so? How can we prevent codependence from becoming so widespread? Think about those things as you read what the researchers have learned.

Family Rules for Codependence

Codependent families live by a well-defined set of rules. These rules are the unwritten laws of their family relationships. Rules operate in everyone's family, but rigidly enforced rules are always present in family systems that produce codependents. All members of the families must abide by the rules, although as with all family rules, the parents have the greatest freedom to change or break them. The exact wording of the rules varies from family to family and so the different writers have reported them somewhat differently.[1] The rules themselves in composite form are discussed below.

It's Not OK to Talk About Problems

This rule first applies to family members in the presence of others. Family problems are not to be talked about with strangers, casual acquaintances, or even neighbors and friends. Nothing should interfere with the illusion that the family is perfect. No problems should be talked about outside the home. Our family is a closed shop. You can almost hear in the background of this rule, "Lie if you have to, but do not talk about us having any problems."

But families unconsciously committed to the rearing of codependent members frequently prohibit discussion about family problems with each other. Requests for conversation with parents about problems are routinely avoided. Standard responses are, "We'll talk about that later," or "There's just not time to deal with that now," or "Now you know you shouldn't be worrying yourself about that little thing." More directly parents may say, "That's none of your business, young man," or "We'll have no bellyachin' about things like that in this house. We're Logans, and Logans don't whine about nothin'."

As a result, the family learns to behave as if problems never happen. If rough water in family conversation appears, it's time for everyone—especially the kids—to disappear. It's time to go do the rest of the chores, watch TV, or sit on the porch. And anybody caught snitching to a teacher, school counselor, minister, or social worker will be cared for in the usual ways the family punishes the disobedient.

This rule is often one that develops a deep reservoir of unexpressed feelings in every family member's storage tank. Anger from a thousand times of being ignored and put down sleeps there. A large chamber in the heart is reserved for the development of shame. If you really do have a problem, and Logan's don't have problems, then any self-respecting Logan would be ashamed. Adults are often quick to reinforce this. "Shame on you Johnnie Logan. Don't you ever betray this family again with your snitching and tattling to your teacher. I've a good mind to whip you to within an inch of your life." Many of us can testify to being closer than an inch away from leaving this life at the end of such emotional and physical cruelty.

Feelings Are Not to Be Expressed Openly

"Don't you come around me with that sweet talk about love. You've got something else in your mind, something you want," and the child wanting to express and receive some tenderness is pushed away for whatever reason. The end result is the child receives the message, Don't express your warm feelings. "It doesn't matter whether you like it or not, whether it tastes good or not, whether you want to eat that or not. Eat it, and do it now!" And the child learns her feelings are not important. She had just as well eat what she is served, do what she is assigned, or go where she is told whether she wants to go or not, and she is to keep her feelings to herself. Otherwise, she will get nowhere in this family. There is no tender ear nor any sympathy. No time for her feelings. To avoid harsh words and even more harsh treatment, she must keep her feelings to herself.

And so suppression and repression become the first line of defense against pain. The addictive pattern is given an early doorway. The way to get along is to keep your feelings hidden. Even when you agree with your parents and want to do things, you are told it's your duty. It really doesn't matter how you feel, what you feel. Keep those feelings to yourself. And if warmth and tenderness are not permitted, don't try any anger, or making with the tears, or being afraid, or having fun. What do you think this is, a carnival?

Someone Else Is Always to Blame for Everything

Responsibility for wrongdoing, mishaps, messes, failures, tragedies, and the like are never to be charged against members of the family. Someone outside is always to blame for bad things. The boss is to blame for Dad's drinking. The terrible situation of his youth, the customers not buying whatever Dad has for sale, the stupid police officer who made a mistake operating that Breathalyzer—those are targetable items for blame.

Of course, Dad may blame anyone he likes. He will blow off steam while he is drunk; but later when he is "better," he will find someone to blame, especially for his own messes. It's awful to hear him blame Mother at first, though. She just takes everything he dishes out and never complains, except under her breath when he can't hear her. Even then, Dad is not really to blame. If only his mother, or his father, or his early chances in life, or his bosses, or if someone had been better to him, Dad wouldn't be in the shape he is now.

Direct Communication Is Mostly Forbidden

Family members use one another as messengers, or other indirect means of communication are selected. This is their first choice for communication. Situation comedy teams in the entertainment world use this process when a third person sitting between two other people is used as a "messenger boy" for communication between the two.

At the supper table, Dad says to his son, "Tell your mom I'm going out with the boys tonight."

Son dutifully responds and repeats the message, "Mom, Dad's going out bowling with the guys tonight."

Mom responds, "You just tell your father he promised to take me to the movie tonight, and he'd better not back out on our first date in six months. And furthermore, young man, stop being a slave for your father. He can deliver his own messages if he really cares about me."

Indirect communication is necessary sometimes, but a constant dose of using others to deliver your messages allows distortion, confusion, and misinformation to creep into every message. Intimacy is diluted, if not destroyed altogether. The family grows to become a group of people who cannot relate to each other or communicate (or miscommunicate) without a third person present.

Do Whatever Is Necessary to Make Us Proud

The negative way to state that rule is understood, "Don't disgrace the family!" Here the emphasis is on the family, not the individual. Children get the message that they are unimportant as individuals; the family group is of ultimate importance.

This is both an internal and an external rule, a right way to do everything in this household. The right way is rarely explained ahead of time, but you just let something be done in a way that does not meet the standard, and immediately the rule will be proclaimed to have been in existence ever since the Ten Commandments. "You ought to have known."

It is important to be good, right, strong, even perfect, and you have to do it in a way to bring honor to the family name. Outsiders must see the family in its best light—and better than it really is, if possible. That will make us proud. And, that is expected. There will be no special medals, honors, or rewards in this family for such behavior. That is expected. However, a codependent family member is not to make the family too proud. To do so would cast a bad light. The boys might show up the father (addict) and cause embarrassment. The girls might progress so far beyond their mother (addict) as to make her extremely jealous. Be good, but not too good. Make us proud, but don't overdo it.

If you fail to live up to this rule, you are obviously an inferior person, an incompetent family member, and a real burden for the family to bear. One ought to be ashamed and will be reminded to retain that shame at every possible opportunity. That will be especially true the next time the family is proud of you. It takes at least ten instances that makes the family proud to diminish one event of shame in a dedicated codependent family.

Don't Be Selfish

This rule is the most universal rule for codependence. You must never put your own needs above the needs of someone else. Good feelings for codependents may only be found (and never spoken about) when the codependent meets someone else's need, by taking care of someone. It is in this way all codependents are able to find meaning for themselves. Their greatest joy in life is to serve others. In that sense, it is necessary for them to find a needy person to rescue in order for them to fulfill their inner calling in life.

Often this is so obvious the codependent person knows about it, talks about it, even makes jokes about it. There is a bit of humor in the way this happens, but it is bitter humor. Instead of being sacrificed early in life to some stone idol and having your lifeblood drained out on a rock on the top of some mountain, you give your blood, sweat, and tears, minute by minute, as a living sacrifice to an addict. In some ways, that's not much of an improvement over the practice of child sacrifice.

Do As I Say, Not As I Do

Children must tell the truth, keep their promises, do their assignments, clean their rooms, take care of their things—especially clothes and shoes that would need to be replaced if they were lost or destroyed—and obey at all times, regardless of the circumstances. The circumstances include potential embarrassment or bodily harm. Always do what is ordered or commanded.

Parents are not required to be a model of this behavior. As a matter of fact, parents may ensure the development of codependent children by breaking promises, leaving their own assignments partially undone, telling white lies, and threatening children with punishment if they tell others about it, and, in general, sending the double message, "Do as I say, not as I do."

Children who behave as irresponsibly as the addicted parent are severely punished. The punishment occurs often even if the child merely threatens to perform in some of the minor dysfunctional ways. The double standard of privileged parents and underprivileged children is always in place. Even the addicted parent is more privileged than the codependent one. Children learn the hierarchical order of family power quite quickly. They also learn they are on the bottom rung of that hierarchy. Self-esteem is penalized in this kind of environment.

It's Not OK to Play (For Poor and Lower-Middle-Class Families)

Life is for doing what is right and being productive. One is not to waste time playing, and that is often true even if the games might lead later to a very lucrative profession. Life is supposed to be "difficult and always painful. . . . this rule lends itself to the development of the codependent view of ourselves as unlovable, boring, stupid, ugly, and wrong. Because of this, the co-dependent must work twice as hard as everyone else just to feel okay."[2]

It's Not OK Only to Play (For Upper-Middle-Class and Upper-Class Families)

Play must not be the entire focus of life; you must have a way to contribute to society to justify your existence. That takes work. Unless you work and contribute in this way, you may live a completely worthless life. According to the low self-esteem script of codependents, this rule reinforces the belief that people are really only worth what they contribute to others.

Don't Rock the Boat

The final rule is that nothing should be done by anyone that upsets the current balance of power, family achievements, or state of family pride. The current balance is most likely an unhealthy one. The more unhealthy, the more pressure there is to keep it the same. Most of the other rules in the list support this last, or summary, rule. If people follow the above seven rules, it is not likely that they will upset the balance. It is most likely that all members will go along with the status quo and begin to act in ways to require others to conform also. The major task of older children is to teach the younger children how to behave in the family system—and to keep them in line. If younger children get away with breaking the rules, the older ones become jealous. If they break the rules and are caught, all the children are likely to be punished in one way or another. Survival requires members of codependent families to stick together and not to rock the boat.

So family rules have been discovered as symptoms of codependent families and as indicators that children of the families will likely become codependent as adults. To add to our growing store of knowledge about codependence, then, we see that a rigid set of rules enforced by parents may force a family to behave in codependent ways and may produce codependent offspring. This seems to be true with or without an alcoholic member present.

Healthy families also use rules, but the rules are mostly open, flexible, negotiable, and designed to help members achieve feelings of self-esteem. While family secrets do exist in healthy, noncodependent families, secrecy is not the general rule of thumb. A whole range of feelings are routinely expressed between family members, and children and parents may openly ask for things they want and wish to have. Others respond with similar openness. Healthy interdependence thrives there, not patterns of codependence.

A codependent person, then, is one whose life can be described as being lived in a pattern. Within the family structure, the pattern follows rules to which rigid allegiance is given. The more addicted to a rigid rule pattern, the more certain the family is to both function in codependent ways and to rear codependent offspring. The exact rules may differ slightly from person to person and family to family, but the general characteristics are remarkably the same. When you know the rules, you can recognize a codependent family quite easily.

Family Roles for Codependence

In almost every family, members share responsibilities. They also develop a place or a role within the family circle. In healthy families, roles and responsibilities tend to shift from person to person according to circumstances and with just about everyone's open support. As with the game "Follow the Leader," each person has a turn setting leadership pace, making suggestions that govern decisions, and actually carrying real leadership burdens as a part of the ebb and flow of normal family life.

With addict/codependent family systems, roles tend to be rigid and fixed. Often trapped by unconscious pressures from other members, each person conforms to the role assigned by the family. At times, the roles are relaxed, but in times of stress the roles are insisted upon with a great deal of energy and intensity. Even when circumstances change, roles tend to remain as they have been assigned. Fathers do men's work, unless they are drunk and cannot. Mothers do women's work, unless they also do fathers' work when they are drunk. The opposite is also true. Mothers may be the addicted ones with fathers doing mothers' work. Children have their assigned tasks and roles too. These roles are so carefully designed it is as if some author wrote out a script to be used.

As early as 1964 Eric Berne's popular book entitled *Games People Play* described a life game of "Alcoholic,"[3] which had several roles including the alcoholic and family members or friends.

Virginia Satir[4] is also noteworthy in this regard because she identified specific roles for family members based on communication patterns. Family members developed into individuals who were

- blamers (who always attacked and focused responsibility on anyone but themselves),
- placaters (who tried to make peace at all costs),
- leveling ones (who were open, flexible, ready to negotiate at all times),
- distracting ones (who never had a serious moment or a commitment they cared to keep),
- computers (who were rigid, factual, and unbending).

Other writers have written about the roles of codependent family members.[5] Ernie Larson identified family roles as caretaker, people pleaser, workaholic, martyr, perfectionist, and tap dancer. The careful researches by the Johnson Institute in Minneapolis identified family roles to be those of protector, blamer, controller, lover, and codependent. Charles L. Whitfield in an early article identified six clearly defined roles: dependent, enabler, hero, scapegoat, lost child, and mascot. He was also among the earliest to stress the need to give attention to professional counselors who played the role of untreated/untrained professional whose desire to help addicts and codependents frequently resulted in misdiagnosis, temporary symptom relief, unsuccessful treatment or treatment failure, and personal fatigue and/or personal burnout.[6]

An interesting list has also been prepared by Timmen Cermak, a psychiatrist who has prepared a book with a main goal to convince readers that codependency is a kind of psychiatric disorder. His list of codependent family members includes the martyr, the persecutor, the coconspirator, the drinking (or drugging) partner, and the apathetic codependent. He implies none are well, and they deserve the medical classification of a psychiatric illness.

Sharon Wegscheider-Cruse[7] says she has discovered six clearly defined roles usually maintained within the addict/codependent system. In her scheme, she has outlined four roles for children in addition to the master pair of roles played by the parents. They seem designed to maintain the rule discussed earlier, Don't rock the boat.

The Addict and the Enabler

The addict's role is called dependent, and the codependent's role is called the enabler. These roles function much as was described in chapter 1 of this book in relation to the alcoholic and his or her supportive spouse. Of special note is the developmental description of an enabler as one who grows into the role by imitating a parent through daily practice. Those who grew up to become enablers were able to learn from and to imitate an enabler to whom they were close and whom they admired—either openly or covertly. Enablers appear to have great patience and an unlimited amount of kindness. Enablers are also seen by others in the chemical dependence field as people whose primary feelings—although those feelings are usually buried, hidden, and out of sight—are in the anger/rage category. Usually their feelings are expressed through subtle outlets, such as nagging; some general unpleasantness that occasionally, but memorably for the children, explodes into fury; frequent and often clever sarcasm; and not so subtle control of everything in sight. Enablers are almost always sufferers of excessive fatigue with an awareness of their ultimate inability to change things. Yet they struggle with the illusion that they can and will change things.

Some enablers develop an active religious life. Among Christians that religious life is frequently expressed as a faith of total submission to a God who will take care of everything. Religious expressions of God giving unusual power that tend to border on unrealism and support the illusion that you will gain power over your family troubles tend to be high on the list of priorities of a codependent's religious thoughts and prayers to God.

If you were a codependent like this, you would tend to believe strongly in miracles and spend a good deal of time focused on the possibility of God making all things right in some not too distant moment in time. The enabler is a classic codependent.

The other four roles are for the children and seem to be standard ones within many families observed. Each child tends to be rigidly assigned to a role. However, all the children learn how to play all of the roles. In small families, children double up on roles. An only child may play one or all of the roles and learn to play each one as well as the other. Some only children have been known to play separate roles simultaneously.

The Hero

Frequently played by the oldest child, the hero is an overachiever. If you were the hero, you would be moved to produce pride for the family and to attract positive attention to yourself. The hero gains self-worth by achievements. Occasionally you become weary because you must work so hard to accomplish what you have set out to do; as the hero, you feel the weight of expectancy from your parents. They want you to succeed.

Younger children look up to you and often relate with pride and imitation. Occasionally, the theme of the relationship becomes jealousy, and the darker emotions related to hatred surface. The usual pattern is for heroes to move forward, showing no emotional response. Praise from siblings brings embarrassment and guilt. Criticism and jealousy bring anger which, when repressed, adds to the guilt carried by the hero. As the hero, you also carry a message that you should never be angry. You will maintain the hero posture at all costs because you must please others. If you are a religious person, you must also please God. When the hero leaves home, other children may attempt to take your place but are never able to fill the bill completely. This adds to the resentment felt by the others and makes homecoming for heroes more troublesome.

The Scapegoat

The scapegoat is usually a role assigned to the second child or other middle children, either sons or daughters. The hero's act is a hard one to follow. As scapegoat, you are usually one of the most sensitive of the children. You feel the pain of the family with a great deal of intensity. In response, you react in ways that draw anger from your parents and condemnation from the community. Whereas the hero brings praise to the family, the scapegoat brings only scorn. The scapegoat has a hidden agenda, however. As Sara Hines Martin says so clearly in her book *Healing for Adult Children of Alcoholics*:

> Another of his tasks is to keep the parents' marriage intact. As long as he keeps them united, going to the principal's office or court, to take care of him, they won't focus on their conflicts. Some examples of Scapegoats would be teenagers who get into dropping out of school, drink, drugs, pregnancy, or running away from home. Although it is hard for parents to see this at the time of the misbehavior, this child has the potential for being the one who is closest to them after the conflicts are resolved.[8]

The major fear with regard to the scapegoat is the tendency to identify with the self-destructive tendencies of the addict parent. To drink alcohol would be sufficiently bad, but scapegoats also tend to destroy their vocational possibilities by sabotaging their academic careers, getting into the drug scene or committing some felony so as to keep them from some job categories. At their most tragic end, the scapegoats tend to prefer suicide to a continuation of a life as it has been.

The Lost Child

A third role in codependent families is the lost child. Some families have children who get lost. This is classically portrayed by a child who is essentially lonely and who deals with conflict by withdrawing. The basic personality type of lost children is to be shy, to spend as much time as possible alone, and to protect their privacy. If you are the lost child, your main goal is to escape the family confusion and find relief "away." This role allows you to withdraw into the quietness of an art form such as poetry or other writing, painting, or sketching. These products are easily hidden even if they are excellent. These forms of escape may be practiced, enjoyed, and hidden from prying eyes.

In this role you may be ignored socially because you do not step forward to make contributions or receive a proportionate share of time. You may be quickly forgotten by teachers even before the end of the school year. Sometimes you do not even show up for class pictures for yearbook publications. Many students wonder where you spent the school years because almost no one remembers having a class with you. At home, the lost child never makes trouble, stays out of the way, and leaves home as a single person as soon as possible to escape.

The Mascot

The final role relates to the hyperactive child, the family clown, the member who seems to know how to have a remark or an antic to take the tension out of the air. Even while being the life of the party, the mascot is basically a manipulator whose activity and constant chatter is an attempt to hide deep personal fear and loneliness. The fun is to deflect attention from the pain and tragedy. If you are the mascot, your fear is that everything around you is going to fall apart. You are well liked by other members of the family. They take pleasure in the fun you create and are glad to be relieved of the tension, if only for a few moments.

Mascots tend to bask in the attention given by others, and because they are usually the youngest child, the mascot usually exhibits slower emotional growth. Mascots seem to be at higher risk for emotional illness. They may also have a tendency toward suicide, second only to the scapegoat.

Adult Family Roles for Codependence

An interesting extension of the study of roles in addiction/codependent family systems relates to the study of childhood family roles as they translate into adult behavior. Marie Schutt[9] traces the role of hero to its adult form of *caretaker codependent*. The eldest, or one of the older children in the family, adopts the hidden rules of the codependent—namely, peace at any price, maintain the conspiracy of silence, never quit, go to any lengths to be right, never discuss feelings, try to seem normal under all circumstances, attempt to make things better with rigid, overachieving efforts, and coddle children as well as spouse in order to lock them into lifelong dependency. Finally, the caretaker codependent displays indecision and creates as much inconsistency as possible. The hero makes an excellent adult codependent.

The scapegoat becomes *the rebel codependent* in Marie Schutt's work. As a child, the rebel used anger to fuel survival tactics. Impatience and frustration, "black moods and bully behavior" were used to manipulate. Shame and blame give energy to criticism and condemning behavior. As adults, these people make demanding marriage partners. While they may well care for their addict spouses, they overpower them in arguments. Even the addict spouse learns it is "easier to give in . . . than to fight." As children, they did not receive parental approval. As adults, they will not give it to their own children. They become angry, controlling parents (more often mothers), and need to see their own part in creating the misery in which they live. Their basic need is for security and assurances of that security, for approval and for evidences of that approval. As adults, they make tumultuous marriage partners. They make as much trouble (or more) emotionally as their alcoholic addict spouses do in their own ways. They are poor risks for happy marriages unless constant emotional warfare is the definition of happiness preferred by their mates.

The role of lost child is translated into one with two masks on either side of the passive way of life. The first mask is the *passive manipulator* who grows into adulthood as a martyr, using others and manipulating them into taking responsibility for decisions. By this method, all responsibility for decisions, good or bad, is avoided. Massive control is exerted on others through this style of life. By her premium on correct, moral, proper behavior coupled with a life of service and overextension she attempts to avoid direct confrontation and be unchallenged for both her passivity and manipulation. She lives a life of fear and indecision.

The second mask is the *passive acceptor*, one who accepts whatever happens as destiny or the will of God. Believing self to be worthless, unimportant, undeserving, this person comes from a home of gross inconsistencies. This person has no ability to say no and probably will stay in a marriage in spite of battering, neglect, and multiple abuses. Addicted partners feel guilt around this person, become frustrated, and are frequently tempted to respond with abuse for lack of perceived options. Children tend to see her as virtuous, patient, even kind, but rather stupid. Then they feel guilty for such thoughts and do not know what to do with the guilt. This person most probably spent much of childhood engaged in fantasy projections and has spent a lifetime believing in magical thinking. She believes her wretched marital situation will magically change. If she is a Christian, she prays constantly for a miracle to change her husband.

The mascot often grows up as a continuously *youthful codependent*. Being reared as the youngest, with pampering and protection, most likely deprived the mascot of learning the basic ingredients of adult life, namely, responsibility, accountability, and self-discipline. Coping strategies of temper tantrums or being cute and acting the clown may have worked long into late childhood, but in the teen years they were resisted by adults. This resistance brought about much sadness, some heavy depression, and perhaps even suicide ideation or gestures during the high school years. As a married adult, the *youthful codependent* remains underdeveloped emotionally and in most ways of maturity. Mascots usually seek a marriage partner to take care of them. They are not real good codependents in that they are "not selfless, and protective and longsuffering." These people cannot be expected to put the needs of others before themselves and do not want responsibility for anyone else's behavior.

Children who are reared with such role expectations and who fulfill them grow into full-fledged codependent adults. Their major competencies in life include keeping themselves miserable, being equal in guerrilla warfare with a marriage partner, and reproducing codependent children to grow into adulthood to continue the tradition.

Adult Children of Alcoholics as Codependents

Discovering that children's later lives are largely determined or at least heavily influenced by their experiences with parents or parent substitutes in their earliest years is not a new insight. It has been observed and taught in the oldest and most revered writings of the human race. It is a part of our secular as well as religious traditions. It was one of the foundation principles of Sigmund Freud's teachings and contributions. It was and is the primary principle underlying modern educational theories, especially the developmental ones. The wisdom literature of the Old Testament is filled with the teaching of the value of parental child rearing.

For example, all of us have three separate states of being in our egos. We have a *parent ego* capable of leading us to behave in ways our parents and other authority-type adults taught us; we have a *child ego* able to energize us to be the child we have ever been or could never be; and we have an *adult ego* able to help us face life and understand reality with increasing maturity—at least to the level of our development. The important thing to see is that these observers of human behavior recognized the power of the child-hood experience of each person to direct adult actions. More than just agreeing with the common sense notion that all of us get childish some time or another, our childlike and our childish feel-ings from the past have a powerful influence on the present.

Another example is clear if you would imagine yourself to be an adult worker on the job. If you were to receive a directive from your boss, you might have two different reactions. Being glad for the work and glad you know how to do that task, you might do it with pleasure because that's what you agreed to do on this job. On the other hand, if your inner child were in control,[10] you might respond with irritation because you are being ordered around. You may resist by dawdling, daydreaming, taking an ex-tra coffee break, forgetting, procrastinating, or avoiding the as-signment in other ways until the boss returns, reminds you, and perhaps has to scold you about your negligence. Nobody wins in this kind of exchange between adults just as neither parent nor child wins very much with similar exchanges in families everywhere.

A good way to compare ACA characteristics listed here with more standard information in the psychological sciences is to look at issues such as parenting and childhood response in the areas of perfectionism, overcoercion, oversubmission, overindul-gence, punitiveness, neglect, rejection, and sexuality.[11] Hope for the ACAs is to help them learn their patterns. They do not, as knowledgeable adults, have to remain locked into them forever. They may learn to make friends with the state of their inner child and learn to include a balanced approach to life using the major values of both the adult and inner child.[12]

Still another look at the problem is the parallel development of a *private self*—the self that is spontaneous, free, open, that loves life and wants to experience it with joy and affirmation—and a *public self*—the self that depends on powerful outside others to direct the self's thoughts and actions. When the child is born, both "selves are equal in size and strength." When the child has grown, the public self is so powerful it keeps the private self under control. This is usually accomplished by a set of rules, assigned roles, or by other means of coercion by significant adults.[13]

Characteristics of Adult Children of Alcoholics

Children, the youngest and most powerless individuals who live with or around alcoholics, suffer the greatest harm. They are often deprived physically, educationally, socially, and in every way one can imagine. However, the most terrible damage is done to the largest number of children in ways that do not show up for sure until they become adults. They develop personality styles and a set of attitudes and strategies to deal with life that penalizes their freedoms, their opportunities, and their personal happiness.

One study identifies thirteen major characteristics common to children who grow up in homes with one or more alcoholic parents.[14]

ACAs Must Guess at What Normal Behavior Is

In their childhood, life was unpredictable. Schedules were hectic, and everything was subject to change on a moment's notice. No normal pattern was ever developed, such as when meals were to be served; when clothes would be washed—or if they would be; whether mother and dad were speaking to each other; whether there would be lunch money for school; whether medical, dental, or other appointments would be made; and so forth. Nothing was on schedule; nothing normal. Feelings were powerfully stimulated but seldom allowed expression. At times, their parents blew up at each other, at them, at others; they learned that sometimes you did express feelings, sometimes not. They did not learn what was normal. They spent so much time hiding, lying about some things, telling the truth about other things, that they lived in a constantly confused world.

As adults, they are crippled. They do not understand normal behavior; and until they begin the hard process of recovery, they make poor risks as marriage partners.

ACAs Have Difficulty in Following a Project Through from Beginning to End

In their childhood, projects beginning with much promise became the family jokes: They were never finished. The doll house is still only a pile of plywood in the basement. The go-cart got the same treatment. The home was filled with empty words, telling of the fantasy of great ideas for the future, the fantastic job to be secured soon, and the promise of the pot of gold, with or without a rainbow. Nothing got finished.

Alcoholics of the wet or dry variety usually demand credit for ideas spoken as if they had already become fully accomplished deeds. It is an addict's pattern to begin, perhaps well, but then not to finish. This pattern seems locked in the memory banks of ACAs and is usually repeated, although unconsciously, in later life.

ACAs Lie When It Would Be Just as Easy to Tell the Truth

This is automatic and universal. Cover-up stories and little white lies became the first line of defense in the alcoholic home. Children told half-truths and lied boldly with parental approval to make excuses for the alcoholic parent. Lies became as natural as physical reflexes. This lingers long into even the most dedicated adult recovery program of ACAs.

ACAs Judge Themselves and Others Without Mercy

Alcoholics constantly criticize their children. Even when the child does well, the effort is not quite good enough. As one ACA told me, his father's highest and most grudging word of praise for him was always, "That's not too bad, for a kid." Everyone receives criticism. When ACAs grow to adulthood, they continue the criticism. Negative self-judgment becomes a nearly inescapable habit. The bad parts of anything are seen as directly their responsibility. "Me, I'm to blame for it all," is the constant cry of the adult child.

ACAs Have Difficulty Having Fun

Memories are clogged with work and the ever-present demand, "Be quiet, don't disturb Daddy. He's feeling bad again." There may be a few big events to remember, a vacation, a ball game, a play, the night Daddy came to the PTA play, but daily home life was mostly without fun or pleasure unless it was private, self-made, and quiet. As adults, fun and games are not on the agenda. Joy, celebration, play, and just turning loose to pleasure are new skills for adult children of alcoholics. Even games are deadly serious competitions; they are battles to win by work, work, work.

ACAs Take Themselves Very Seriously

This characteristic is linked with the "no fun" observation. To do anything that might "make me look like a fool" would be enough to keep the ACA glued to a chair. One must not open the self to ridicule. Life is a very serious business.

ACAs Have Difficulty with Intimate Relationships

Of course, adult children of addicts do not have the corner on this market. Intimacy is difficult for a large variety of persons in the American society, but it is especially true of this group. Honesty, openness, trust, with one's feelings and commitments in terms of relationships, is often temporary. Today's children have great difficulty with intimacy. Their major problem is they have never seen a vital, healthy, intimate relationship. They remember wanting intimacy with their parents who gave them a double message: first a tender message, "come close," followed by a harsh one, "go away." Codependents were loved today and rejected tomorrow; they worried whether parents would love them tomorrow under today's conditions, or whether they would have to work overtime to figure out the proper (and new) conditions for acceptance tomorrow too. Children of alcoholics were always wondering whether punishment from past offenses would con-

tinue for weeks or months and whether they could trust a promise
of "forgiveness."

Besides, if parents are lying, as they do so often; if you depend
on them and they let you down, as they do most of the time; if
they abandon you and love someone else, what's the use of risk-
ing intimacy. Children who are not the recipients of healthy love
and do not enjoy consistent commitment from trustworthy adults
grow up as adults who are tentative about relationships. They not
only have difficulty with intimate relationships, they are not intimate and are afraid to attempt to be so.

ACAs Overreact to Changes Over Which They Have No Control

Growing up with no control left an unresolved fear of being
out of control within this group of people. No one likes the out-
of-control feeling, but under normal circumstances, healthy
adults recognize they can relax and not have to be in charge of
everything each moment. ACAs must be very controlling, rigid,
and mistrust spontaneity just to survive. They often show their
anxiety by attempting to control everyone in their vicinity, telling
them where to sit, how to sit, what to say, interrupt them when
they are speaking, telling them not to do what they obviously had
chosen to do. And if a mere wish, request, or demand won't bring
about the control, then less subtle means, such as bribes or depri-
vations, are attempted. Anxious ACAs try to reassert their balance by control of themselves and as many things and people
around them as possible.

ACAs Constantly Seek Approval and Affirmation

In childhood, these adults often subsisted on low diets of approval and affirmation. In addition to trying to catch up, they
have very few ways to know where they stand with others around
them and are seeking to be sure everything is OK. They are always alert for anything that looks or sounds like it might be a
compliment. A surprising twist with this group of people is that a
sincere and unsolicited compliment is difficult for them to accept.
In an extreme case, anyone giving praise is likely to be written off

as ignorant or worthless. Who would be so stupid as to compliment such a worthless person as myself? the ACA reasons.

ACAs Feel That They Are Different from Other People

This is more than just understanding yourself as a unique person. If you are an ACA, you feel awkward, not able to fit in with the others. Having missed a normal childhood and teenage life, you believe, with some truth, that you do not look at life the same way everyone else does. You can't carry on conversations like others can. You have nothing to talk about. This characteristic is related to the desire to remain aloof from others and is an added reason to avoid the deeper levels of friendship and intimacy. It makes so many others of these characteristics stronger.

ACAs Are Either Super Responsible or Super Irresponsible

This group of people has a radical relationship with responsibility. They either assume total responsibility for everything, or they refuse to take over anything. There is no middle ground with them. Cooperation and teamwork is not a part of their preferred way of life. The responsible type continues to pile work upon work and seems unable to say no to anyone. They are actually afraid someone else will find out they are phonies; or they just don't want to have to work closely with anyone else, so they'd rather do it themselves. The irresponsible ones use the same reasons to support their decisions not to be responsible. They do nothing so they won't be found out to be phonies; they also won't have to work with anyone if they don't work.

ACAs Are Extremely Loyal, Even in the Face of Evidence That Loyalty Is Undeserved

As children, relationships within the family were established on the bases of family loyalty and so-called love that existed in spite of the presence of addiction and bizarre behavior. Family members were cemented by fear and insecurity that was overcome largely by loyalty to the rules laid down by the parents. Such a lifelong covenant developed strong capacities for loyalty.

In addition, friendship is usually a difficult task for an ACA to achieve. Trust to outsiders is not given easily. For that one reason alone people from ACA families sometimes never seek the assistance of counselors and appropriate helping professionals with their addicted family member, not to mention their own personal needs. However, once a friendship is established with an addict or an ACA, that friendship becomes a treasure. No matter what the friend does or says, it is just too much of a treasure to part with. Besides, the known friend has demonstrated loyalty to you, so you can trust her. No matter how poorly she treats you, you will remain loyal. It is too great of a loss to reject the friendship just because of hard times. After all, what may appear to be a hard time to outsiders is certainly not a hard time to you; you are a veteran of several past wars and can take a little roughing up to preserve a friendship.

ACAs Are Impulsive

Being impulsive leads to confusion, self-loathing, and loss of control over their environment. In addition, they spend an excessive amount of energy cleaning up their messes; and even in this task they move about in compulsive activity. They are unpredictable, sometimes inappropriate, and uninhibited. After all, if they have no sense of the normal and anticipate you will be loyal no matter what they do, you can expect them to do almost anything. Given the fact that they also can't believe you really care for them, they are out to test your friendship; and they may resort to extreme measures to test you.

Other Characteristics of Codependence

Almost every single cluster of characteristics of a codependent person, which becomes a leading edge of that person's way of meeting life, is related to the master image of codependency, that of *caretaker*.[15] Almost everything listed at any time seems to be directly related to a desire to take care of something or someone other than themselves. Actually, when seen from the proper angle, almost every single action or activity relates to self-care.

They feel anxious, guilty if they don't do something to help, and pity others in need. Those feelings are inwardly painful. They help others, in part at least, in order to reduce those awful feelings within themselves. Codependents do not as a usual rule feel secure or safe. But they feel the safest when giving to others, helping others, and providing for the needs of others. They feel the cleverest when they can anticipate the needs of others and then meet them. This satisfaction is perhaps the most positive self-praise codependents will allow themselves, but then usually only for a fleeting moment.

Codependents must really be on the job, because as worthless persons their most serious claim to a valid life is in the taking care of others. The self-care dimension is present, but the codependent is not conscious of it. She says, "I'll do thus and so for Johnny so he will like me." Then, when Johnny says, "Thank you," or even "I like you," the codependent says to herself, "See, he likes what I do to please him, but he doesn't like me, so I'll just have to try harder."

She has met her unconscious need. She believes she is not likable. So she has twisted Johnny's words around in her mind to make him say that he likes what she does, but not her. She has served herself quite well, and defended herself from even low-level intimacy with Johnny at the same time.

Overreaction

A most frequent codependent personality characteristic is a pattern of overreaction. Everything is a crisis. Codependents actually "feel bored, empty, and worthless if they don't have a crisis in their lives, a problem to solve, or someone to help."[16] Even a little thing is converted into a big deal. When someone needs or wants something, codependents will stop—even leave—what they are doing and rush to the aid of the person asking for help almost as if they were EMS workers on the way to help a heart attack victim. This style of codependency often develops excellent crisis-oriented skills and can function well in a real crisis. But the difference is the codependents (1) often offer assistance when not requested, (2) send a boatload of aid when a postcard to express friendship would have been enough, (3) keep on thinking, worrying, and being upset about matters long after the true crisis is past, (4) experience much discomfort when there is no crisis; in fact, codependents may invent or cause a crisis, may relive a past crisis, or may anticipate a future crisis in a simulated anxiety attack if they cannot be placed in the middle of a real ongoing one.

Codependents tend to make a major production of a simple task. They react to a perceived slight by declaring all-out war—often demanding spouse and other family members shun or otherwise punish the person whose only crime was not to speak to them in the post office this morning. They make big plans for a publicity campaign, a job that could be managed quietly with two or three phone calls; they exaggerate almost anything if given half a chance. They keep people around them on edge because like a battleship in a war zone their defenses seem always on "condition red." Codependent persons love to work in the church where people in charge of things do not plan ahead and have to have their programs rescued at the last minute by the whirling, swirling codependent crisis crew.

Low Self-worth

Codependents do not have a corner on the market for low self-worth, but it is one of the most universal parts of their personalities. Those reared in alcoholic families are ashamed of their alcoholic parents. If they were reared in rigid rule-following families, they have learned to lie and cover up reality with half-truths and lies. They believe they are not as worthy as others are and certainly not worth as much as others. Even those codependents with obvious talents and skills believe they are not good enough. They reject praise; compliments make them feel uncomfortable. They become extraordinarily anxious when promoted too far at work or if they are nominated for high office. They feel their lives are worth very little, and they attach themselves to others or to some vital cause to give themselves some reason for living. Most of their feelings that look like self-worth are artificial in that they are derived from those to whom they are attached.

Codependents believe they do not deserve happiness, that good things or the good life should not come to them or that they could not really be loved by others. People who say they like them or love them are either dumb or are just other worthless persons like themselves. Yet all the while, codependents try to prove they are good enough; and they work all day and overtime to prove it.

One would think that a codependent person would be open to understand the Christian teaching about a God who sent Jesus Christ to take care of the needs of all humans. However, it is actually difficult for them to believe that. If there is a God, they reason, that God must be pretty stupid to make such a sacrifice for such worthless persons as themselves. God may sacrifice for others, but not for people so undeserving as themselves.

Controlling

Control is a key characteristic of a codependent. A codependent person insists on being in control of as many things as possible. This actually is a reaction against feeling that they, the codependents, and their lives are being constantly controlled by events outside themselves and by other people. They have a history of pain and suffering when other people control them. They have seen what terrible things can happen if others are allowed to do as they please, so they attempt, in conscious and unconscious ways, to control the important people and things around them.

They frequently exert control through manipulation and employ a series of tactical maneuvers to get their own way. They live lives of planned helplessness. They pretend to be helpless to see if anyone will try to help them. They will alternately try to intimidate, skillfully use guilt, directly give advice in a friendly manner, or use threats as the situation requires. In any event, the codependent becomes skillful in being in charge of the way things are done and how they are accomplished.

Probably, more codependents are disliked due to this characteristic than any other. Sometimes their antics are seen as cute. In older persons they may be passed off as eccentric. But in each case, the people manipulated begin to build up a reservoir of frustration and anger toward the codependent because of this dominating characteristic.

Boundary Violators

Codependents are unaware of normal structures, and that applies especially to personalities. They frequently do not recognize when or where the territory of another person's life begins and their own ends. They cross over boundaries forcefully with their children. Frequently, on the pretext of being helpful, of rescuing a needy person, program, or project, they crash into a situation that is obviously none of their business, and make their chosen contribution without bothering to ask permission. They are greatly irritated or offended when other people insist on privacy or personal territory. They will overreact and end relationships with people who do not allow them to cross boundaries regularly. They call them snobs.

Poor Communicators

Codependents are hampered because of their inner personality styles, but they are crippled mostly due to poor communication patterns. They are afraid of openness, directness, honesty, and other characteristics of intimacy. They use extreme measures in communication: they blame, threaten, bribe, beg, coerce, and use sarcasm. They rarely say what they mean and mostly do not mean what they say. They take themselves very seriously, but do not expect normal, ordinary persons to take them seriously. They would never ask for what they want or need. They would rather manipulate to secure it. They have difficulty expressing their emotions with honesty. When anxious, they speak so as to confuse others. They talk too much, and they never say no, even when it is fairly obvious they cannot comply with the request being made. They will die trying!

Two dyed-in-the-wool codependents who married each other would have massive communication problems. They would be like the pair of vultures in the movie *Jungle Book* trying to decide how to spend an evening.

"What do you want to do?" asked the first bird.

"I don't know. What do you want to do?" said the second bird in reply.

"I don't know," solemnly returned the first bird.

Whereupon a third bird, obviously not a party to their codependent attempts to please each other—not bound by the secret pact they had not to offend each other, and not willing to stay locked in indecision rather than take a risk to voice a personal thought or preference—said, "Aw, shut up!"

Codependents stay locked into the unhealthy dimensions of their relationships due to their deep underlying personality characteristics. But those characteristics are revealed clearly in the way they do or do not speak to each other during the course of their lives together.

Several additional characteristic patterns are easily identified for codependent persons. *Lack of trust* is a prominent one. Codependents rarely trust other humans or systems designed by humans, and they are even tentative in their trust toward God. Most surprising of all, they do not trust themselves, so they do not have a base to trust in anything or anyone. Codependents as individuals also experience *sexuality as a major problem area.* Of course they are not the only ones to do so. But one can hardly imagine a codependent being a warm, open, and affirming sexual partner. Sexuality is a problem for codependents because they are persons with low self-worth. They want to take care of a sexual partner's need whether they have simultaneous needs or not. They frequently cannot voice personal wants or needs. They live with high levels of shame, guilt, and anger. They are afraid of losing control. They often feel sexual revulsion toward their mates; and they lie about or make up reasons to abstain instead of using direct messages like, "This is just not the time for this kind of intimacy."

Codependents also live with one or more *obsessions.* They live with a much-practiced ability to use *repression* to avoid uncomfortable thoughts and feelings. And, they major in the reality destroying practices of *denial* and *avoidance.* These are not unusual characteristics when taken alone. They are characteristic of many different kinds of unfortunate, unhappy, or unhealthy behavior known quite well to physicians and counselors. However, one or more of these characteristics favor the codependence diagnosis when it highlights a personality already addicted to finding meaning only in relationship to other persons.

Rescue Oriented Professionals and Codependency

It may come as a surprise to you, but doctors and counselors themselves are likely to be suffering from a problem their patients or clients are having to battle. Counselors and doctors are just as likely to come from dysfunctional or chemically dependent families as any other group in our society. Actually, because doctors and counselors are professional helpers, there is a high degree of likelihood that codependents would be especially drawn to those kinds of jobs. Some estimates place the possibility of helping professionals who are codependents, in at least a mild form of codependence, to be nearly 80 percent of all those practicing.

For a long time, doctors and other counselors in many disciplines were barely introduced in their formal training to the best strategies for providing appropriate care for clients who were alcoholics or members of the families of an alcoholic.[17] Such training as well as personal therapy is now generally available. When you seek assistance in the task of recovery from codependence, it would be well for you to inquire from the person referring you for counseling as to the specialized preparation of your counselor. Both educational preparation and therapeutic attention is necessary to prepare a well-rounded therapist.

For those who may not know what you may mean about specialized preparation, you may direct them to two ideas. First, let them read this succinct comment:

> *If therapists hope to help clients understand co-dependence as the serious dysfunction it is, then those recovering from their own co-dependence must be willing to take steps to heal themselves first.* Whether this takes place in a

Twelve Step program, in therapy, or both, it will take a substantial time and dedication—often as long as two years or more.[18]

Then tell them of a second matter of preference, if indeed it is a preference of yours. Since recovery is basically a spiritual process, then a counselor who is a person of spiritual maturity or at least one who will respect your own faith and use it actively in the therapy would be a better therapist for a Christian to consult.

Summary

Our travels have brought us to a wider definition of codependence. No longer just a compulsive helper related to an addict, or a person whose internal needs require him or her to rescue others in order to find personal worth or value, codependency has become a broad-range category of family malfunction with several types. It may be generated by second or multiple generations of this kind of person by passing it on to their children. Evidences of such training centers for future codependents include the discovery of closed families who live by rigid, restrictive, personality-altering rules; families who require members to follow carefully scripted roles of a particular nature; families who are dominated by some of the major codependent characteristics and pass them on to their children.

Codependency also may be detected by observing the children to see if they suffer from any or a pattern of characteristics on the list discovered in the Adult Children studies. Children with ACA patterns are definitely codependent and will, if married, live out a codependent marital script and rear codependent children. A careful look should be taken at members of the helping professions, especially the counseling-type professions. Many of its practitioners are codependents, but the nature of their daily tasks masks their addiction to codependent life-styles. They are paid to be codependents in our culture. They rear codependent children.

In passing, careful note should be taken of a central core of characteristics developing around the definition of codependent.

Each category of codependency studied has the following characteristics in common:

- low self-worth, an intense need for someone else,
- an illness-producing way to deal with guilt and shame,
- dislike of or fear of intimacy,
- poor communication skills,
- a closed or covert life-style with family and with neighbors,
- an absence of functional spirituality, including an inability to trust,
- a powerful urge to control in a covert way,
- self-protection as a central goal, which overrides all morality,
- craving for tenderness and affection, yet an inability to deal with it if it is available,
- a set of broken relationships with no method of relationship repair,
- an enormous amount of pain at deep levels,
- extreme loneliness,
- a lifetime inherited pattern of behavior that may very well be changed by spiritually based therapy!

Certainly there is some kind of relief for such large masses of people who are injured and in such deep pain. The next chapter is focused on the good news of hope.

Notes

1. The researchers seem to have taken the rules from listening carefully to the families and deducing them. It is also obvious that some of the earlier writers have been copied by later writers, but much of the time no cross-references are given. These references are selected. Robert Subby and John Friel, "Co-dependency—A Paradoxical Dependency" in *Co-Dependency: An Emerging Issue* (Pompano Beach, Fla.: Health Communications, 1984), 34-43; John Friel and Linda Friel, *Adult Children: The Secrets of Dysfunctional Families* (Deerfield Beach, Fla.: Health Communications, 1988), 54-57.

2. Subby and Friel, 40.

3. This game was briefly described in chapter 1 of this manuscript.

4. Virginia Satir, *Peoplemaking* (Palo Alto, Calif.: Science and Behavior Books,

1972), 59 *ff.*

5. "Why Haven't I Been Able to Help?" (Minneapolis, Minn.: The Johnson Institute, Inc., n.d.), 4-9; Ernie Larson, *Stage II Recovery: Life Beyond Addiction* (Minneapolis, Minn.: The Johnson Institute, Inc., 1985); and Timmen L. Cermak. *Diagnosing and Treating Co-Dependence* (Minneapolis, Minn.: Johnson Institute Books, 1986), 4-5, 36-40.

6. Charles L. Whitfield, "Co-Dependency: An Emerging Problem Among Professionals" in *Co-Dependency: An Emerging Issue* (Pompano Beach, Fla.: Health Communications, Inc., 1984), 45-54.

7. Sharon Wegschieder-Cruse, "Co-Dependency—The Therapeutic Void," in *Codependency: An Emerging Issue* (Pompano Beach, Fla.: Health Communications, Inc., 1984), 2.

8. Sara Hines Martin, *Healing for Adult Children of Alcoholics* (Nashville: Broadman Press, 1988), 29.

9. Marie Schutt, *Wives of Alcoholics: From Codependency to Recovery* (Pompano Beach, Fla.: Health Communications, Inc., 1985), 23 *ff.*

10. W. Hugh Missildine, *Your Inner Child of the Past* (New York: Simon and Schuster, 1963).

11. Ibid., 67-69.

12. Ibid., 284-89.

13. Subby and Friel, 31-44.

14. Ibid., 24-54; Janet Woititz, *Adult Children of Alcoholics* (Pompano Beach, Fla.: Health Communications, Inc., 1983), 4.

15. Melody Beattie, *Codependent No More: How to Stop Controlling Others and Start Caring for Yourself* (New York: Harper and Row, 1987), 37.

16. Ibid.

17. Anne Wilson Schaef, *Co-Dependence: Misunderstood-Mistreated* (San Francisco: Harper and Row, 1986), 7.

18. Cermak, 94.

3

What Does the Bible Say About Codependency

Codependency takes Christians by surprise. It exposes a central Christian theme, like "service to others," and demonstrates how you can have the best of intentions and yet can be unwittingly destructive in your desire to serve others. We are startled to realize that the actions we intended to use to produce something good got twisted around and actually produced something evil.

Codependency really shocks Christians. Just when you think your faith has helped you to avoid problems others must endure, you discover that Christians are vulnerable to many of these things also. And not only are Christians likely to be involved in the most common illnesses of the body, they are also vulnerable to codependence, one of the most prevalent personality disorders in our century. And it takes Christians just as long as others to achieve recovery.

This may be because many secular or Christian codependency workers do not know how to make good use of the spiritual strengths of the Christian faith in the struggle to recover from codependency. Perhaps this is true because we Christians have not been bold enough to declare the parts of Christianity best able to be mobilized to provide help in such a struggle. It's senseless to accuse non-Christian clinicians for not knowing how to help when some Christians and Christian ministers do not know the best ways to nurture true Christian spirituality. We do not know the most satisfying ways to assist ourselves or others to discover and follow God's will or to befriend fellow believers in a properly steadfast way as they attempt to achieve full and autonomous freedom within the gospel. This chapter is designed as part of the homework Christians need to do in that direction.

But first, a disclaimer. Since the days of Simon the magician (Acts 8:9-24), Christianity is and has been vulnerable to misuse. What is offered here is not for casual application by Christian codependents or by those who would befriend Christians in their struggles to recover from codependency. Here you will find no quick-fix remedies for Christian codependents. Here is an initial response to some of the general themes of codependency from the sources of the Christian faith, but mostly from the Bible itself. They are offered in the prayerful hope that Christian codependents and those responding to them will be able to see the seeds of spiritual power available in Christianity for wholesome, healthy, happy, and fulfilled living. And it is hoped these seeds will be used in ways to enrich the spiritual lives of codependent persons.

Codependency is a counterfeit experience.[1] It attempts to substitute for intimacy and masquerades as an authentic existence. Codependency constantly takes the good and uses it for evil ends. So, the first step toward recovery is to be in touch with the Spirit of God for discernment to see the difference. The next steps in recovery are also spiritual in nature.

A first step will be a brief look at some selected biblical materials. In looking at these materials, I will be working from a limited perspective. The Bible has a great deal of depth and meaning as it shows the strengths and weaknesses of people. Therefore, to concentrate on the codependent elements of biblical individuals and families means to leave out some of the positive elements. As we look at these biblical accounts, don't forget the limited perspective of our look.

Old Testament Materials

A brief reminder of family stories in the Book of Genesis reveals the codependent patterns with remarkable clarity. These brief, truthful, open, and honest presentations in the Bible are models for Christians in the ways we can look at and describe our own family lives as we seek healing and recovery. Although *code-pendency* is a new term to us, codependent behavior can be seen in the Bible.

The Story of Adam and Eve

The Bible begins its account of human life with the story of Adam and Eve (Gen. 3:18—4:26). In this story of the beginning of human history, Adam and Eve were created with a capacity for intimate relationships with God and each other. Notice how they at first thrived within their intimacy with God and then avoided and rejected that intimacy. Having also broken their original covenant with God, they next refused to accept the blame for their part in the break. They converted whatever guilt they felt into shame. Their lies and half-lies did as poor a job as their fig leaves in their attempt to cover themselves and to blame someone else for their failures. In the process, they alienated themselves from God, from each other, and began a clear pattern of avoiding responsibility and reality.

Do you wonder that with such parents the children should worry about being cared for? Cain, their firstborn, became the family scapegoat, not the hero. Feeling unblessed, he murdered his brother, the second-born Abel. The Bible here presents the first human family as dysfunctional, unable to deal with deep negative feelings except in the most drastic and murderous ways.

The Stories of the Patriarchal Families

In later stories, (Gen. 21—38) the dysfunctional style continued. Abraham, known as the "friend of God," demonstrated intensive favoritism to his son Isaac and basically rejected Ishmael. Abraham blessed Isaac with the family wealth and heritage. When Isaac became an adult, he too played favorites. Esau was selected as his favorite son, while Jacob, Esau's twin brother, became the favorite son of his mother. Two family triangles were established. The family became greatly dysfunctional and operated in patterns based on lies and deceit.

When Isaac approached death, Rebecca successfully plotted

with her favorite son, Jacob, to deceive the aging and blinded Isaac and to steal Esau's blessing. Esau was enraged and planned to murder Jacob. Rebecca reported Esau's murderous intent to Jacob, and Jacob fled the country. Rebecca never saw her favorite son, Jacob, again.

Away from home, Jacob lived with his uncle Laban where he used his skills to outwit the uncle out of much of his wealth. He married two of Laban's daughters. When relations were at the breaking point with Uncle Laban, Jacob returned to the land of his youth. During the escape from Laban, Jacob's favorite wife stole the family gods from Laban's worship tent. She hid them and lied to keep the items she had stolen.

The Bible does not tell us what had been happening with Esau. We do not know how far he may have come in forgiving Jacob. We do know that time is a great healer. However, it is unlikely that Esau had forgotten his greedy brother who had stolen his birthright and his blessing. Nevertheless, Esau had done well with the "lesser blessing" Isaac gave him. Now Esau was on his way to meet Jacob.

Why did Esau bring "four hundred men" (Gen. 33:1) with him? Did he want to impress Jacob with his clout? Had he planned more than a welcome to the Promised Land, then changed his mind? Did he want Jacob to know that he could not manipulate his way out of meeting Esau on his turf? Was Esau committed to have the upper hand and therefore brought his power with him? Perhaps we will never know for sure.

We do know that Jacob was afraid of Esau (32:11). We know that Jacob did not depend entirely on God for his safety. He seems to have decided to bribe his way into Esau's favor (see 32:13-21). Jacob also separated his family into four groups for their safety. In doing so, Jacob favored Rachel and Joseph (33:2). It is to Jacob's credit, however, that he moved out in front of his family and faced Esau.

Esau ran to meet Jacob who had bowed to the ground seven times (33:3). Instead of harming Jacob, Esau "embraced him, and fell on his neck and kissed him, and they wept" (v. 4). God had placed forgiveness and reconciliation in Esau's heart. Jacob recognized this by saying to Esau, "To see your face is like seeing the face of God, with such favor have you received me" (v. 10; see 32:30). This must have been very difficult for both of them given their codependent life-styles.

The act that assured Jacob of a measure of Esau's forgiveness was his public acceptance of Jacob's lavish gift (see 32:13-21; 33:8-11). By giving this gift, Jacob found his way back into the good graces of his twin brother. Esau's acceptance must have meant some measure of reconciliation between the brothers. His acceptance of Jacob's gift was an acceptance of Jacob. Thus Jacob knew reconciliation with God and then with his brother all within twenty-four hours.

Jacob and Esau parted peacefully. God had obviously worked in both their lives, although we are not sure of the depth of their reconciliation. Jacob promised to follow Esau home after refusing Esau's offer of an armed escort (vv. 12-16). However, the old Jacob lied to Esau. Instead of following Esau home as promised, Jacob went in the opposite direction. Even God cannot help codependent people in a short time. It took years for Jacob to live up to his new name—Israel.

But the biblical writers were not finished with this family. Jacob's family grew, but the inherited flaw of extreme favoritism continued. Jacob chose Joseph among his twelve sons as his favorite. He spoiled Joseph with lavish gifts beyond those of his brothers. Joseph the child was arrayed in the badge of his father's favoritism, his coat of many colors. Joseph appeared to be immensely arrogant. Even his dreams depicted his brothers in a subservient role to him. It is easy to see how his brothers could hate him. As a boy, he took an overlord posture toward them. So, they awaited their opportunity, which came in the wilderness. Only the action of a softhearted older brother, Reuben, saved Joseph for slavery instead of immediate death.

The openness of the biblical record to present these stories with their imperfect people is remarkable. The flaws of the characters reveal their kinship to people of all generations. These were not perfect people. God did not give them special instructions so as to enable them to live exemplary family lives. They exhibit the dysfunctional styles and codependent characteristics of any ordinary family of any century.

The Story of Lot

The Bible also shows more aggressive and abusive styles of addictive and codependent behavior. Abraham's nephew, Lot, is depicted in a most blatantly abusive activity (Gen. 19:1-38). In the months following the destruction of Sodom and Gomorrah, Lot's daughters took upon themselves, the story records, to rescue their father from social disgrace. Lot was without male heirs, also a mark of God's disfavor in that era. The daughters, according to the biblical story, each in turn seduced Lot with wine, made him drunk, and each became pregnant by him in order "to preserve a people for him."

These drunken and incestuous acts are not less reproachable as family behavior because they occurred in biblical families. Nor are they to be normalized because they are reported to have been voluntary or initiated by the young women themselves. The daughters are reported not to have been forced to bear their father's children. The fact that their sexual union produced two separate peoples, the Moabites and the Ammonites, does not remove the abusive facts of the case. This was clearly an act of incest. This activity of female children caring for a father's need is as sinful as it is boldly codependent. And all of this in the context of drunkenness; it is a poor attempt to reduce the responsibility of Lot, as if one is not responsible for what one does when drunk. Certainly this was a clear example of codependent behavior.

The biblical narrative has never attempted to coverup indications of family malfunction, to hide the clear and blatant lies family members speak to each other, to mask the gross dysfunction of biblical families, to gloss over murder or incest. On the contrary, they are in the Bible as a record of the trustworthiness of the God who wishes to communicate at all levels, of His willingness to be engaged with us and to invite communication with us in our inner beings. They are in the Bible to invite all people to use its pages not to look for some human perfection, but to discover that even these early people needed spiritual assistance, needed to find their help in God. It is incredible to discover how many people still believe they cannot confess shameful deeds to God, as if God would be discovering such terrible human activity for the first time!

Other Relevant Old Testament Materials

Codependent patterns are visible throughout the Old Testament period in many additional places. Selected examples have been chosen here. Having escaped the slave pits of Egypt, the Hebrew people are reported to have turned quickly to the reestablishment of the worship of idols (Ex. 32:1-24). In this story, Aaron, the brother of Moses and the priest of the new Hebrew religion, acted as the chief engraver of the golden calf idol. When caught in the act by Moses, his lame excuse was to blame the people and to say he threw the gold into the fire, "and there came out this calf." This sounds incredible to a healthy person; but to a codependent addict, it is a quite acceptable excuse. Aaron did not lose his priesthood, however, in spite of his participation in leading the nation in idolatrous worship.

The great commandments presented by God to Moses (Ex. 20:2-17) and then given by Moses to the people for strict observance relate directly to codependence. And they represent the heart of the Hebrew faith. The first two of these Commandments deal directly with a prohibition against worshiping any God but the Lord God of Israel and against the using of or conceiving of any image or idol to represent God. Idolatry was not permitted. The very root issue related to codependence was declared to be sinful as early as the Ten Commandments.

Two separate interpretations based on those commandments were developed throughout the history of the Hebrew religion. This was not the intention of God but a fact of Jewish history.

First, a legalistic system was designed: a system of temple worship connected with a series of rules and regulations. If you wished to be religious, you would keep the laws and bring sacrifices to worship in the temple according to those laws. The more perfectly you kept those laws, the more pleased, so they taught, God would be with you. As followers of the law, according to the priests, you would be within the Mosaic covenant with God and continue to be numbered among the faithful. In that manner, a Jewish person would be assured of religious status before God and in human worship.

The other strain, a more pietistic system, was kept alive mostly by the psalmists and prophets. This more interior way of keeping the law involved faithful observance of the covenant, but also encouraged worshipers to seek God in spiritual ways while still remaining within the community of faith. God was to be sought for God's own self. Hebrews who would do so discovered God at new levels of personal religious fulfillment. In the prophetic interpretation of the Hebrew faith each believer was considered to be ultimately responsible for his or her own life choices or ways of living. This line of understanding is stated most clearly in the writing of the prophet Ezekiel. (See Ezek. 18:1-32.) As believers, Hebrews were instructed that they were not locked into a system of penalties where they became responsible for the sins or guilt of their entire family, nor was the whole family required to pay for the sins or the guilt of one of its principal members. Each believer must stand responsible before God for individual sin.

The prophetic strain also taught that religion included the inner self, the heart, and not exclusively the external self, the actions and obedient responses of believers to rules or regulations. True religion involves knowing and believing in one's heart that there is a God, a God who loves and cares for each person, and a God who can be known by anyone in the privacy of his or her inner self. The clearest summary of this new faith is given in the memorable passage of the new covenant in Jeremiah.

I will put my law within them, and I will write it upon their hearts; and I will be their God, and they shall be my people. And no longer shall each man teach his neighbor and each his brother, saying,

"Know the Lord," for they shall all know me, from the least of
them to the greatest, says the Lord; for I will forgive their iniquity,
and I will remember their sin no more (Jer. 31:33-34).

Action and relationships follow from love and gratitude and not
from external coercion and legal requirement. One day, the
prophets promised, God would send a redeemer to deliver the
people from all known kinds of bondage.

But the years passed. The interpretation of the prophets re-
mained in the background, and the people grew weary of the increased power of the priestly caste. The legal system was declared the way of the faithful. The people waited for a release
from the obligation to obey the law and all of its many interpretations. They eagerly awaited the coming of the promised messiah,
God's redeemer, who was to usher in the new covenant so eagerly
proclaimed by Jeremiah and others. For Christians, Jesus Christ
was that Redeemer.

This statement of the two interpretations of the Commandments is admittedly simplistic and overdrawn but basically true.
For instance, the opposition between the prophets and the temple is not clear cut. Some prophets and psalmists worked in the
temple. Yet there were those faithful people who kept alive the
more spiritual elements of the covenant from which came the
prophets and psalmists who sought to correct the abuses of the
temple. God sent messengers continually to call the Hebrew people back to the heart of their historic covenant. Those messengers and their messages were mostly rejected. Finally, even God's
Son was rejected.

New Testament Materials

The New Testament reflects a clear picture of the biblical religion at the time of the birth of Jesus and as He grew to maturity as
a religious teacher. During this time, the legalistic party was in
firm control of religious faith and practice. Great lists of religious
rules for the living of daily life had been developed for the people. Believers were taught to keep these rules perfectly. The sys-

tem of animal and cereal sacrifices based on the Old Testament had been harnessed as a form of religious taxation. Its revenues of tithes and offerings were used to support the temple, the priestly families, and the synagogues. The system was a heavy burden on the people.

Before and during the earthly life of Jesus, a large group of wealthy Jews seemed able to survive and to keep the law exactly. They supported the system, and the system met their needs. It should be noted that these religious leaders believed in what they were doing. They understood their brand of legalistic religion to be from God. They were very sincere in what they lived and advocated for others. The masses of people had no voice in this, and in their poverty were able to fulfill only the most modest parts of the law. But the rich and fashionable citizens enjoyed the best of everything and religiously claimed the blessings from God that such obedient servants as themselves ought to have deserved.

In many ways, the practice of religion had become a matter of form and ritual. To qualify as worthy before the religious law, a synagogue member would have to obey strict rules about family activities, personal diet, daily life, and religious devotion. They had to attend a large number of services and make many sacrifices. They had to make generous gifts of at least a tithe to the synagogue and temple each year. They had to support special feast occasions too. General charity as well as caring for elderly parents, widows and orphans, and for society's unfortunates— the crippled, blind, deaf, insane—also had to be managed. Religious credit was given by the rabbinic teachers to those who rescued the needy. There seemed to be no escape from these burdens. By means of this system of religion, the priests and rabbis introduced more, rather than less, stress to the lives of the people.

Not all of the Jewish religious leaders were for legalistic religion in opposition to Jesus. Men like Nicodemus and Joseph of Arimathea are examples. Also Acts 6:7 says, "And the word of God increased; and the number of the disciples multiplied greatly in Jerusalem, and a great many of the priests were obedient to the faith." It must be noted that the greater number of converts of the wealthier Jewish classes came after Jesus' resurrection.

Into this environment Jesus came. He opposed religious legalism forcefully. He taught that religion was first a matter of the inner spirit. Outer relationships with other people were to follow the leading of this inner faith. Religion was never to be reduced to a code of laws to be obeyed. His message proclaimed the good news of God's loving forgiveness. Religion was *for* people, not against them.

> The Spirit of the Lord is upon me,
> because he has anointed me to
> preach good news to the poor.
> He has sent me to proclaim release
> to the captives
> and recovering sight to the blind,
> to set at liberty those who are
> oppressed (Luke 4:18).

His message was not well received by the religious establishment. But the overburdened people heard Him gladly. Jesus called people to a deeply powerful form of interior spiritual religion. He attacked the religious teachers as those who "load men with burdens hard to bear" while the priests themselves "do not touch the burdens with one of your fingers" (11:46). He clearly rejected the marketplace interpretation of religion. On one occasion, Jesus acted out His feelings with great effect. In His only recorded act of physical rage, He attacked the commercial money-changing stalls and animal-trading booths within the temple compound itself with a whip made of rope. He drove the merchants and money changers out of the temple, at least for that one day (see John 2:13-16).

And He called the people to the spiritual worship of God, to worship God in Spirit and in truth. (See John 4:23-24.) Jesus placed Himself directly in the messianic and prophetic line by referring to Himself openly as "the way, the truth, and the life," for this life and for eternal life, as the "bread of life," and as the "light of the world" (John 14:6-7; 6:35; 8:12). He boldly called the people to Himself, saying, "Come unto me, all ye that labour and are heavy laden, and I will give you rest." Here His reference was clearly to a different religious style than the extreme legalism to which they had been accustomed. Jesus invited them, "Take my yoke upon you, and learn from me; for I am gentle and lowly in heart, and you will find rest for your souls" (Matt. 11:28-30, KJV). Clearly and definitely, He opposed legalism and championed a faith of grace and forgiveness.

Here was an alternative to getting religious benefits by doing things. One is not justified before God, Jesus taught, by keeping the commandments nor because one belongs to a certain family. Here was a different way to be religious. Here even the wandering and straying children who had removed themselves from the worship of God for any reason could return. Even if they were prodigals, believers never were to be viewed as "hired servants" or "slaves." As in the famous parable, they are welcomed into the fold of God as full heirs, as children of God (see Luke 15:11-24).

When you believe in Jesus as the Christ, the Son of God, you do not join some human family. You become a member of the family of God. Jesus taught us God is like a kind parent whose "good pleasure it was" to provide the kingdom for the rightful heirs (Luke 12:32). As a believer you have become a newborn child of God in the Spirit of Jesus Christ. You have been forgiven your sins; you live life now without God's condemnation. You are one of God's heirs. Gone is the shame carried since the beginning of time, and gone is all of your shame: all of it carried by you from the beginning of shame's invasion of your person. As a believer in Christ, you live in a state of not being condemned. (See John 3:18.) You live in the delicious state of freedom from all that is negative. You are a receiver of the love and blessing of the grace of God through Jesus Christ. Codependence tries to block this out of your mind, makes you think it is not true, but it *is* true.

These themes are taken up and amplified in the rest of the New Testament. The apostle Paul's Letter to the Galatians forthrightly declares the freedom of the believer from legalistic religion.

"For freedom Christ has set us free," said Paul in triumphant language. And then more soberly, "and do not submit again to a yoke of slavery." Any keeper of the law is bound to obey the whole law, he stated. That is an impossible task. No one can do that. But when you are "led by the spirit, you are not under the law" (Gal. 5:1,18). You are in a spiritual relationship with God. Codependence attempts to convince you that freedom in Christ is false. It tries to have you believe you want to help or rescue everyone in sight as a Christian duty. This is a false reality. "For everyone must carry their own burden" modifies the idea that we are to "bear one another's burdens"(Gal. 6:2-5). Nurture where nurture is appropriate and necessary, but allow each one to carry a proper share of the load as he or she is able and has agreed.

Free Christians live by the Spirit of God as God's own dear children, for "When we cry, 'Abba! Father!' it is the spirit himself bearing witness with our spirit that we are the children of God, and if children, then heirs, heirs of God and fellow heirs with Christ" (Rom. 8:15-16; also see 1 John 3:2-3).

A key to Paul's interpretation of Jesus and the Christian faith is to be found in his teaching about salvation by grace. "By grace" Paul said, "you have been saved through faith, and this is not of your own doing, it is the gift of God—not because of works, lest any man should boast" (Eph. 2:8-9). After receiving the gift, you live your life in spiritual companionship with Christ, a relationship Paul frequently described as having Christ actually dwell within you (see 2 Cor. 5:17). In such companionship, you practice spiritual awareness of Christ's gracious presence. You attempt each day to become more mature as a Christian. Christianity teaches that you may achieve an intimate relationship with God through such inner and heartfelt communion with Christ. Through faith in Christ as the Son of God, you experience spiritual rebirth and become God's child with all the rights and privileges of God's heirs. This comes as a free gift of the boundless love of God. It comes as a result of God's grace. It includes forgiveness of sins and hope of spiritual life for you right now and for eternity.

Application of Biblical Principles to Codependence

Much of what is said in the Bible relates directly to codependence. The importance of this to you, if you are a person who functions as a codependent, relates to whether or not you want to use the biblical faith to help you to break the power of your addiction.

Remember, the power of your addiction to hold you is very strong. The best way to break addiction's power is to join your spirit with the powerful Spirit of God. As you grow in God's Spirit and grow toward God through the Bible, you will discover the joy of regaining some control of your own life. And you will leave the falseness of codependence behind.

At this point, remember that the awesome forces leading you and others to a codependence addiction and then holding you there are also spiritual forces. But those forces are not good. If they were good, you would not be experiencing all the trouble you are having now. Those forces actually try to lead you away from God.

One way codependence attempts to keep you in its power is to encourage you to dismiss the very idea of spiritual power as foolish. Many people say spiritual power is just part of your imagination. But the power of codependence is real, spiritual and powerful. And codependence does not have your welfare on the agenda. You have been engaged with the spiritual side of codependence, and that's how you got hooked into it in the first place. Without God, a person is no match for an evil spiritual power. Sometimes, with God, people are no match for an evil spiritual power because they have not exercised the spiritual side of their faith. You probably agree with me that if God's power is stronger than codependence, it has to be the greatest spiritual power available in the universe.

You are correct about that: God's power is the greatest spiritual power available anywhere. And God's power has been known to energize people through personal relationships with God when combined with concepts from the Bible. Together, the relationship with God and the Bible can help you become free from codependence. If you follow biblical truth, you will discover just how powerful these truths are. In my spiritual view, they are profoundly simple. I believe they are and will continue to be of great help to Christian codependents. A Christian theology for codependence may be written out much like the following:

God is Spirit, and the only way to relate to such a God is in your inner heart. But the biblical teachings also include ideas that serve as symbols and images to guide the spiritual relationship between yourself and God. The first of these idea images is that the spiritual God is *Creator* of everything that is, including human persons. And everything created is *good*. God intends everything to be for good, but people often become spiritually influenced to use good for *evil*. In spite of this, the Creator God *loves* all persons. God celebrates your existence and eagerly wishes a spiritual relationship with you. God hates *sin*, which is anything that interrupts your relationship with Him, destroys your fellow humans, or destroys yourself. God hates the sins you do, but God still loves you as a person.

With a God who loves like that, it is incredible that low self-esteem has a chance to develop among humans at all. The idea that we are not worthwhile is an example of how we choose not to listen to God. Actually, to believe that we are not esteemed after we have the love of God and learn through the Bible that we have received the *blessings* of God is one of the major evidences that there is *evil* in the world. Each person is of great value and worth to God. Each of us, the Bible asserts, has been created in the very *image of God*. We pass that image on to our children, but for some reason, we do not pass on God's blessings as well. We have received, enlarged, and passed on every *curse* we can imagine to our children, all the while pleasing the *evil one* with the personal curses we have kept for ourselves. And we have fallen for the false suggestion that we just might find our lost identities in the lives of others. If we serve others, a good religious kind of activity, perhaps we can discover our being.

The Bible teaches that *it is in God that we live and move and have our being.* The heart of the codependence addiction is the attachment to another person in order to find ourselves. That is *idolatry.* Nothing is to replace God. When we relate as a codependent attached always to others, we avoid God; we become functional atheists. Christians are free to serve others, but we are to do so in ways to enrich them and not to enslave or control them; and we must not do so in ways to destroy ourselves.

But God does not abandon us in our sin. God has sent *Jesus the Christ*, the only begotten, unique Son of God into human life to reveal God's own self to us; Christ was *God in the flesh.* By placing our *faith,* that is, our complete trust, in Christ, we participate in what has amounted to humanity's second chance to establish a spiritual relationship with God. We *confess* our sins to God through Christ, and God *forgives* those sins when we confess them, and God forgives freely by *grace.* Through God's gift of the Christ combined with your faith in Christ your sins are forgiven and forgotten in God's grace, never to be counted against you again, not to be kept as badges of shame. You are restored to full possession of God's image and are *born again* as a child of God, an heir of God, and a member of God's own family. That status does not admit to low self-esteem. Your environment, your history, your friends, your neighbors, and even your families may insist you are worth little, but in God's eyes, you are a very important person.

You will discover much about yourself that seems sinful. You do not always behave like a child of God. For example, a person caught in the codependent pattern will either unwittingly or on purpose attempt to control loved ones, to play God for them. The Bible invites you to surrender this and your other such sins, your shortcomings, and all of your deficits to God, and to do so on a day by day basis. The word *surrender* is used because it implies you give up all your evil intent but keep all of your abilities; you are still a worthy and able child of God. You are still the blessed, born-again child of God who may surrender both your sin and your desire to sin into the hands of God. Like the great apostle Paul, you may not be able to do everything you wish to do, you may not be able to keep yourself from doing the things you do not wish to do; but in a day by day relationship with God, you may surrender those newfound parts of yourself as you discover them. This is different than the Greek concept of submission, one in which you "give up" as well as "give over." God wants you to remain able, to develop yourself and your gift to the highest possible level. And God wants you to be quite ethical as you go about it.

You are to behave in ways that bring your gifts and abilities to *maturity*. This Bible word is often translated as "perfect." In the Bible, one was expected to be a perfectly good, that is, a mature and able adult. This did not imply moral perfection as we have come to understand "perfect" today. People did not in biblical times, nor do people now, arrive at a place and time when they were absolutely without spot or blemish in action or morals. That is not possible. People do, however, become mature and full grown. And even full-grown people make mistakes. Then the Bible says, "If we confess our sins, he is faithful and just, and will forgive our sins and cleanse us from all unrighteousness" (1 John 1:9).

And so when you are tempted to demand "perfection" of others, remember to hope for their maturity. And when they fail, hope for grace to have a forgiving spirit. And hope to be treated by others like that. Codependent persons can profit spiritually from understanding a true sense of maturity instead of dwelling on a false sense of thinking a Christian can arrive at a state of moral perfection.

Life will become real for you as you fellowship with the Spirit of God, day by day. Celebrating life's joys and blessings, confessing and finding forgiveness for your blunders and sins, and in the constant relationship of the grace of God, you will have peace with yourself and be at peace with others.

This profoundly simple style is enormously difficult, very complicated, but very possible. And it is possible because of the great grace and love of God. It will be available to you one day at a time, but only after you choose to seek God in faith through Jesus

Christ to establish a truly spiritual relationship with God.

For Christians, the route is the same. Be restored to the joy of your salvation in Christ, and then through Christ, seek a truly spiritual relationship with God. And seek out a competent Christian spiritual guide.

Usefulness of the Codependency Model to Christianity

The development of the codependency model has caused Christians to focus their attention on addictions, and especially relationship addictions. It has helped us to see how all addictions, and the codependence addiction in particular, affect individuals, families, small groups, churches, ministers, and the way the churches go about the day by day activity of ministry. The codependency researchers have also theorized about the ways in which codependence affects our political and cultural lives.

We can now see that the faith itself and the way we may practice it often allows codependent persons to continue to be codependent. It permits codependents to transmit their patterns to others. We have seen how codependence is sometimes responsible for some of the disruption in our churches and its various organizations. We have seen and heard that Christians of all ages are susceptible to codependency and its patterns.

We have seen codependence as a problem passed down through the generations by way of families. Now we need to pay attention to the patterns of family life our church has and realize we will be transmitting these patterns to following generations as well. Knowing the patterns used by codependent persons and having some methods of interrupting the cycles of those patterns have given Christians a valuable set of tools to combat codependence. It does not need to remain such a powerfully destructive force within family and church life. Trial and error methods can now be avoided because of the careful work of some codependence researchers.

It is also encouraging to have a system made up mostly of secularists to insist that the only workable answer for the recovery of codependents is by using a spiritual method. The massive

amount of funds and human resources poured into the traditional types of care, both public and private, for alcohol and substance abuse have always brought a low percentage of recovery
by any measure. But that is doubly true when traditional types of
care are compared to the twelve-step programs (see ch. 1), which
are basically volunteer and based on spirituality. Codependency
programs based on spirituality have shown excellent results with
chemical dependents and their families and show early promise
with codependents. Christian counselors report good results using recovery models compatible with the Christian faith in their
counseling. Christians, especially the leaders in the churches,
have been given an excellent example of the power of the Spirit
when harnessed to the task of challenging codependency and encouraging human development.

Christian Concerns About Codependency Programs

In addition to the many positive contributions made by those
involved in the codependency movement, there are some con-
cerns about codependency to be voiced by Christians. I hasten to
add that I have not read all of the materials in print. But the generous sampling I have read brings me to make the following
comments.

First, many of the codependency writers and workers seem not
to understand the place of appropriate nurture in human relationships. So much attention is given to stopping codependents
from playing at the game of rescue that it seems to be forgotten
that there are some times when a codependent person may legiti-
mately care for and provide for the needs of a marriage partner.
The ordinary need of spouses for nurture, of children for tenderness and care, and of the general population for the "milk of human kindness" is often overlooked. Requiring alcoholic partners
to fend for themselves when they are drunk, especially when they
are having withdrawal symptoms or "the shakes" from coming
off alcohol without medical help can be life threatening. Actually,
a cold turkey withdrawal may be a life and death situation—an
emergency. Statistically, upwards of 15 percent of the alcoholics

who come off alcohol cold turkey and develop delirium tremens have died. To preserve the lives of alcoholics and the well-being of the codependents who would have trouble forgiving themselves if their loved ones died, it is better to call the EMS or otherwise summon proper medical persons in an emergency. To require alcoholics to ask for or to bargain for what they need or to negotiate as independent persons in such a crisis is its own kind of abuse.

Second, there is little clear mention that the twelve-step programs (see ch. 1) are positive or substitute addictions. This is certainly not a negative comment in the least. The positive addiction of following the twelve-step programs is a helpful focus for lives otherwise dedicated to addictions that produce negative, tragic, and destructive ends. To live by these twelve rules for the rest of your lives, good rules to be sure, to be required to attend or to be encouraged to attend a minimum number of meetings over the first year, and also to change both traffic pattern and companions as such activities require demands quite a strenuously focused new set of habits.

The point I want to make is that the process is a change of one addiction, a destructive and negative one, for a positive one. It is, in my opinion, good for the person to know about and to affirm this change—to celebrate the substitute addiction, to make the new pattern as much an activity of rational and volitional choice as possible. The process of recovery makes use of the addict's illness pattern to forge the changes, but the basic structure of repetition, routine development of habits to replace the old ones, and strongly suggested or mandatory attendance in remedial meetings is heavy into an addictive pattern itself. It is also heavy with a legalistic style. Reinforcing the change, focusing on the positive with reinforcement, and celebrating the open choice to do so is of importance in relapse prevention. The more the recovering addict is able to participate in the changes and to affirm a commitment to positive addiction, the better the chances to prevent relapse.

Again, therapy itself has been known to become a substitute

110 CODEPENDENCE AND THE CHRISTIAN FAITH

addiction; and therapists are to be aware of the need to nurture
autonomy in their clients and counselees. Unfortunately, all
sponsors do not have the discipline, training, or moral restraints
all of us might wish.

Third, little attention has been given in the materials available
so far on the *nature of forgiving others*. Such activity does not come
easily and does not stay put when given. Being one who has been
abused and who in turn has become an abuser is a serious plight
in which to find yourself. How can you preserve yourself from the
debilitating hatred you would have if you kept anger sealed in
your heart against those who have abused you? How could you
possibly deal with the shame that would accumulate if you constantly rehearsed in your minds your guilt concerning those you
have injured, coupled with the anger you have toward those who
taught you how to do it. Forgiveness by God, by others, and by
yourself are all important ingredients of spiritual survival. Your
forgiveness of others is also an important skill; forgiving others is
a survival task for yourself.

Next, little is said in much of the codependent literature about
depression, with the exception that codependents are often de-
pressed. Some of the lists of symptoms of codependence mention
depression, but many do not list its most recurrent form: grief.
Necessary grief work throughout the recovery process is vital to
the codependent person. The constantly occurring and reoccur-
ring waves of depression that become the lot of a codependent
who begins the process of recovery deserves attention. If you as a
recovering codependent person worry about the deliverance of
your addicted loved ones, reassure yourself and take heart. You
will be strengthening their self-esteem when you cease your excessive rescue activity. You will also be amazed to see how your
relationship with your loved ones improves and matures.

Again, the spiritual nature of dependence is a challenge not yet
addressed by codependence writers. As an addiction, codependence is an overattachment. As a way to derive meaning for a
person with low self-esteem, it has classical theological overtones
related to one's own being. Thinking about your own being is not

a new theological idea. Thinking of your own being as if it were possible only as you are in a relationship to another human person is simple idolatry. There is much to assist a truly open codependence researcher who might have an interest. Exploring this side of codependence as it is related to human spirituality seems vital enough to be done soon.

Besides, how does any person expect to escape from a dilemma such as codependence without the assistance of a thoroughgoing spirituality? If you as the codependent are directed to seek out the Higher Power best known to you, how can you keep from falling into the trap of relating to "the God of the hodge-podge of random impressions" that you collected from a lifetime of trying to avoid religion? How can you avoid the alternative God of your previous teachings, which you have rejected forcefully? How can you escape the God of some other strong personality near you that lands you right back into the codependent trap from which you are trying to escape? In addition, by a focus only on the God of your impressions today, you ignore your own religious history and a mature resolution of that history, and you also ignore the possibility that others who look to you for spiritual leadership might also ignore theirs. Rejection of all or parts of one's religious history after careful, prayerful, and mature consideration is far different than doing so in a spirit of adolescent rage. In almost everyone's religious history, some item of useful value for mature and independent life exists. To find it and put it to use strengthens a person's will to search for new and more worthwhile spiritual values. To reject one's religious and spiritual history out of hand often trivializes both religion and spirituality at one or more levels in people's minds and hearts, making their use less than potent as useful allies to cure powerful adversaries like patterns of codependency behavior.

In the process, you may be one of the persons who may ridicule the set of images and symbols used by Christians in their religious practice and spirituality. I as one Christian ask you to listen to what has been found to be true within the Christian faith. Spirituality is not possible for most people without some sort of images or symbols. Except for a few rare saints, symbols are very necessary. Two thousand years of religious history in the Christian tradition have taught us at least that. It is not possible to have a spirituality without some symbol for God, some symbol for evil, some symbol for sin, some symbols for dealing with the challenging terrors of human life, such as pain, betrayal, loneliness, illness, injury, and death.

In my small practice I have counseled with codependent persons who have gotten burned out on a rootless, symbol-free spirituality, one without religious or ethical moorings. I have celebrated with them when they have gained a measure of freedom from abuse, struggled with them in the early phases of autonomy and responsibility, and then agonized with them when the very people who had been such liberators and models turned on them in abusive and unethical ways. The high priests of the God-as-you-know-God-best faith gain the advantage of not forcing a sectarian religion on people, but they also face the deficit of possessing a temporary spirituality unfit for the longer haul of life. That anemic spirituality seems unfit to provide stability and safe mooring for the needs of recovering addicts and codependents in the major crises of life. A spirituality is unfit to be relied on that cannot provide a believer with a firm basis to meet and successfully confront the challenges of evil in its many passive and aggressive forms.

Finally, I wonder if the uncritical spirit concerning their own work displayed by many of the codependence writers has been pointed out to them. Of course, they have the latest new model of human behavior to present. They have the inside story about a new set of symbolic patterns of human behavior. Human experience immediately supports much of what they say. However, that has been true of every new thing to come along in every decade. Their blanket dismissal of most of the work of psychiatrists, psychologists, clergy, and others are key indications to me that their own formulations of their findings are probably going to be short lived. If lasting contributions are to be derived from the codependence research, as well as the model itself, then the researchers, clinicians, and the writers will do well to discover ways their new insights about human nature reinforce and blend with or challenge and alter the body of commonly understood, tested, and tried understandings. They will also offer their findings with carefully researched conclusions. And they will do so in the places where they may be in open dialogue with knowledgeable others in the give and take of the open forum of learning. Hopefully, they will soon get off the hobby horse that the whole world will have to regroup themselves to view everything through codependency glasses.

But they may not choose to do so. They have made their contributions in their own ways. They will doubtlessly continue in the way they wish. I am grateful for the good work they have done. I am hopeful for the kind of balance and maturity that will make their work more permanent, more usable, more mature.

The next chapter indicates a way in which codependent Christians and others may use counseling resources to sustain a worthwhile program of recovery.

Notes

1. For a discussion of this theme, see Adrian Von Kaam, *Personality Fulfillment in the Spiritual Life* (Denville, N. J.: Dimension Books, 1966), especially chapter 4, "Counterfeit of Religious Presence," 123-53.

2. As generally taught and practiced in the Hebrew faith. See Joshua 7:1-26.

4

How Do You Get Help for Codependency?

If you are codependent, you are encouraged to consider the following:

- There are people who understand pain like yours. They are willing to stand by you if you want to recover.
- There are parts of yourself fully able to gain enough strength to begin to recover from codependency.
- There are ways you can claim your spiritual power, regain your personal authority, and begin to recover.

Spirituality is the place to begin to recover from codependency. And only a spiritual path will be able to deliver you from the ravages of alcoholism, chemical dependency, or codependency.

Magic is not spiritual.

Magic or whatever else promises to whisk away a problem or a trouble in the twinkling of an eye will not be helpful. It may give you a temporary high, but a magical solution will have you to come crashing down in a hurry.

The hallmark of magic is instant success. To make magic work, you must trust a human being who stands between you and the great power. You must trust some person who graciously tells you what to say, what to do, who performs the correct ritual, and who promises to take all the pain and strain of life away. Whoever offers you a simple, magical solution to your addiction offers you something that does not exist and cannot exist except in a life of fantasy.

Aware people have known for a long time that there is no cure for alcoholism. But there are hundreds of hospitals, clinics, and institutes with doctors, counselors, and other personnel who have programs designed to help alcoholics dry out and to assist codependents to find spiritual center so they can work on some processes to help them recover. Churches, their counseling centers, and their many departments and agencies also have people and equipment increasingly better prepared to provide the proper assistance for your recovery program.

I repeat this another time as a caution and an additional opportunity to make the point clear. An alcoholic may stop drinking and by some means stay sober, and so no longer be drunk again. You may become a dry alcoholic, but you will still be an alcoholic. Usually, one drink is all it will take, and you will start the addictive process all over again. Soon you will be back among the ranks of the wet alcoholics. This is true of any alcoholic said to have recovered. And that is also true of healings closely linked together with religious conversion.

Even these converted persons will still have many of the same features of the alcoholic personality. They will still have the cravings for alcohol. They will still behave occasionally, if not frequently, in strange and addicted-like ways. They will not be just pretending to live out their drunken patterns. They will always be recovering alcoholics with all the struggles and temptations known to any other alcoholic.

But recovering alcoholics are enormously improved human beings. Any one of them is like a modern-day Lazarus: resurrected from the tomb of drunkenness. And, if those alcoholics were already believing Christians, they will be better Christians. If they had not been believers before and in the process of recovery came to faith in Christ, then they have won the prize of spiritual life here and hereafter as well.

What has been said about alcoholics is equally as true for codependents. There is no complete and total cure for codependency. Once the codependent habits have become part of your personality, they will always be stored up inside your memory in some measure or another.

But, you can become a recovering codependent. You may discover and continue to discover strategies and methods to defeat the most harsh effects of codependence. If you are mildly codependent like so many are, there is a great likelihood that you can get much better even though you will still have the codependency patterns planted in your heart and soul for your lifetime.

Even if you are severely codependent and may also be addicted to a variety of behavior/substance additions, there is increasing hope for you as well. Counseling methods and training programs based on spirituality have been and are constantly being developed and improved. And, they are available to you to assist you to become more independent, autonomous, and less under the direct influence of your codependent patterns. In the vast majority of these programs, spirituality is the point to begin. Remember, a recovering codependent is remarkably different and more healthy than one who is just an unaware codependent.

A recovering codependent is much like a modern Elijah; after escape from the cave of self-pity, that old prophet continued his recovered life under the leadership of God.

- He was restored to a place of honor by God.
- He was given new life and new hope.
- God gave him at least three new jobs to do.

As a recovering codependent, you will have enormous energy released to focus on the new tasks of living life with joy. You will now be free to be creative and productive in ways you scarcely dreamed you could be. Former relationships with people will be free to become warmer and richer. Your faith in Christ can be stronger, and your joy in serving the church can become more honest and forthright, more rewarding and pleasurable.

As a recovering codependent, you will have developed close associations as well as intimate relationships with some genuine and trustworthy friends. Thus, if you have a relapse, they will tell you about it pronto. Then you, and they together, will work to see you restored to your recovery plan. As soon as you are able, you will take the lead yourself, assuming responsibility for yourself, beginning again to have the spiritually healthy, independent refreshingly free set of good feelings you love again. You will refuse to slip into the old ruts and stay there. You will have learned about the joy, freedom, and peace there can be in recovery. You will want to remain in recovery and not in codependence all over again.

As you can see, recovery is not a matter of magical action. It cannot come overnight. In this case, faith alone will not get the job done. The recovering codependent must live every day, one day at a time, from faith to faith. Remember magic is just another form of idolatry. It must be rejected along with any tendency to worship idols of wood, stone, and metal.

As you might imagine, one of the main purposes of this book is to encourage persons who may believe they might be codependent to seek some guidance, some counseling, perhaps some therapy in order to begin a spiritually healthy plan of recovery. This, or course, will be for your own benefit and for the benefit of those around you. The following pattern outlines some steps in a recovery plan. It is a standard plan, but a very possible one. It combines the best possible features known to me for such help.

Please hold in mind my opinion that it has taken you all your life to develop your patterns of behavior. It will take some time and a lot of energy to make some changes, even for the better.

Some persons today insist the only things needed to recover are a few lectures, a study course or two on codependence, and maybe some practice in the area of improving your self-worth or self-assertiveness. These can be excellent things to do. I encourage everyone interested and able to do so to attend such sessions. However, they are bound to be sampler exercises. They will give you glimpses of what might be if you would just participate in a recovery plan of your own. Such lectures and speeches might lead to frustration unless you make a plan that begins with your own personal needs. If you really want to recover, you need to follow these steps: (1) you will have to decide to recover; (2) you will have to begin from where you really are; and (3) you will have to follow through as long as it takes to finish the plan.

Remember, it is a major codependent characteristic to begin a project and then not to finish it. Your very codependent self may sabotage your plan.

There is at least one surefire way for Christian persons who suspect, or know for sure, that they are codependent to seek out competent help and to design and follow through with a recovery plan.

First, surrender (as opposed to submit) yourself to God. Second, confess your lack of power to solve the codependency problem yourself and ask the Lord for guidance. Third, commit yourself to the task of recovery with the help of God one day at a time.

Move from there into a trusting relationship with a counselor prepared both in the areas of spirituality and codependence therapy. Then give yourself enough months or years to make steady progress in your own recovery. Pray often. And listen for the feedback from the people around you.

Some folks will like your new genuine way of relating. They will like your honesty, your faithfulness to your promises, your taking responsibility for yourself. Some will even like the refreshing way you expect people around you to bear their own burdens and be responsible adults.

Others may say you have changed. You are not as friendly, they may say. If they mean they cannot manipulate you into doing their dirty work as they used to do, if they no longer can pull the wool over your eyes and fool you about things, if you call their hand about lies and the like—if these things are true, then take their comments about you not as criticism but as compliments.

Such negative comments will hurt. It hurts to have others say harsh things about you. However, you do not have to fire back as good as they send. Just insist on telling the truth, keep your promises, and continue to recover. The friends you make among other recovering codependents will be deeper, more steadfast, and more spiritual than these manipulating kinds of folk. Besides, these controlling kinds of acquaintances may come to themselves, realize they too are codependent, and seek recovery for themselves.

First Step in Recovery[1]

The first step in recovery is actually a three-step process in one.

Learn the Features of Codependency as a Pattern of Behavior

The first part of the first step involves learning the features of codependency as a pattern of behavior. You need to see codependency as a destructive pattern that injures people and infects their own ways of relating. It involves your looking at the individual characteristics as well as the patterns. It involves you in the task of comparing these codependent characteristics with the style of life lived by healthy people. You will be well on your way when you can see how these characteristics and patterns bring unhappiness to the persons behaving that way, the mates they live with, and most of all, how it affects their children.

Getting a good picture of codependence means understanding some of the symptoms like those described in chapter 2 in this book. Any time three or more of these symptoms are part of anyone's behavior, then that person probably is codependent.

Allow Yourself to Recognize Symptoms of Codependency in Your Own Life

The second part of the first step is to allow yourself to see whether some of the symptoms of codependency are a part of your own way of living. You yourself do some of these things. As incredible as it sounds, you probably really do some of them. Here it is important to see whether or not your version of those symptoms is beyond the normal bounds for those kinds of behavior. Helping people and even rescuing them when the situation calls for it can be quite a normal thing to do. You are not codependent just because you have a nurturing personality. This is especially true if the persons you help are helpless, or nearly so. It is very important that you make a careful distinction between providing assistance to persons with legitimate needs and insisting on helping those who do not want to be helped. It is also a good test to check out whether you are helping in such a way as to make these people dependent on you from now on, or whether your helping will enable them to help themselves more ably in the future. Parents are to provide things for their children that they need but cannot provide for themselves. However, when the children grow toward maturity, parents begin to step back and nurture increasing independence in their children. It's a difficult thing to do, of course, but even teenagers need "enough support to know they have not been abandoned while getting enough freedom not to be smothered by their parents."[2] This is normal and healthy parenting. At times it is quite frightening to see our children having to face the temptations and challenges that face them today, but there is no way to grow up for your child.

The codependent kind of helping is very different. Codependent helping is rushing to someone's aid more in order to meet your own needs than to meet theirs. It is you helping because for some unknown reason you feel you must help—you feel driven to help—and the intensity may be completely unconscious. You know it is unconscious when you can't give a good reason for helping. When the reasons for your helping rise out of your need to control, and when helping may be against the will of or without the invitation of the person being helped, it is probably a codependent urge. Be aware that some helping of others, some feeding of others, some care for others may be quite normal. It is the compulsive, uncontrollable urges to help that are indications of codependent behavior. But, when you come to see some of these symptoms in your way of living, and when you see several of the symptoms form a pattern, you admit to yourself that you are probably at least suffering a mild case of codependence. And then check out the other symptoms of codependence shown in this book. As you identify yourself in these patterns, you may be ready for the next part of step one.

Or you may resist readiness.

Nothing is more certain than your tendency to deny you are a codependent. However, for some people the denial will last no longer than ten seconds. You will realize it is obvious to most that you are codependent. The symptoms all describe you exactly. So you are ready to move ahead.

For others, however, the denial is intense. It may take enormous energy to break through it to admit to yourself, even in the private space of your own mind, that you are a person with codependent symptoms. You may fear losing your old identity if you were to change. You may fear losing your grip on yourself if you have to start over emotionally and intellectually. You will try to convince yourself it isn't worth it, it isn't going to do any good; you may deny having any feeling one way or another; so why bother?

Then you know. The only way to go forward is to take a leap of faith. After all, change and recovery from anything in this life is spiritual in one way or the other. There is no sense denying your spirituality. It is there even if you haven't thought about it. If you wish to escape the pain of codependence and protect those around you from the damage inflicted by your codependence, you must begin your recovery. To begin, you must confess to God and yourself, "I am a codependent."

Admit to Another Person That You Are Codependent

The third part of the first step is to admit to another person that you are codependent. As you might know if you have attempted to do it, uncovering and admitting require strength, courage, self-trust, and faith in others of a high order. That is a difficult assignment for a codependent person.[3]

A friend, a pastor, or counselor may have led you to know about codependency and have helped you to apply the definitions to yourself. After you have passed through whatever feelings you have generated toward that person, whether they be irritation, anger, shame, or even guilt, remember how much that friend must care for you to have done this for you. After getting over the initial shock that someone else can see what is going on inside you, still cares for you, and still wants to help, I hope you will pass on to the next step rather quickly. The quicker you move to step two after admitting you probably are codependent, the more rapidly you will actually begin a healthy recovery.

You may desire more convincing, however. Choosing a place to begin within yourself may be important to you. You may wish to begin with some additional self-help. Several codependents insist on that. I suggest to codependents that their desire for more information before beginning to work on the process of recovery may just be one more evidence of their codependent behavior. It may be the erupting volcano of control, one of the most insidious patterns of the codependent armament resisting any effort toward healing. I still encourage investigation and involvement in self-help. However, I encourage that be done at the same time a person has beginning conversations with a counselor. For self-help enthusiasts, I encourage you to write to Codependents Anonymous, P.O. Box 33577, Phoenix, Arizona, 85067-3557. Identify yourself as a newly discovered codependent and ask for a starter kit to help lead you to the road to recovery. You may be able to find a Codependents Anonymous group meeting in your locale. Begin attending soon. Recovery will not overtake you immediately, but the friends you make in such a group should be people who will befriend you no matter how long your pilgrimage will last. You may also want to secure something else to read. Select some things from the suggested reading list in the back of this book, if you wish, but be sure to look at Andrea Wells Miller's *Breaking Free: A Workbook for Facing Co-dependence.*

For Adult Children of Alcoholics, be sure to have a look at Janet Woititz's book by that name. If one or both of your parents were addicted—overeating, workaholism, gambling, etc.—be sure to review the characteristic personality traits of ACAs in chapter 2 of this book.

These introductory materials are full of information and are written in easy to understand language. Anything written to give you information about codependency from a reliable source will help you in stage I. You may also want to check out your local hospitals and health care centers where programs for alcoholics and chemically addicted persons are traditionally available. They nave begun to offer public lecture series on the features of codependency. The hospitals and clinics in my own Louisville, Kentucky, area offer an excellent series of public information presentations on chemical dependency and codependency. They also offer full-scale treatment facilities for chemically dependent persons and their families. Such public places are other excellent sources of good information about codependence. These places also know the names and whereabouts of some well-trained codependent counselors in your area too.

More and more, pastoral counseling centers in hospitals, colleges and universities, and others supported by church groups, such as United Appeal, have begun to give attention to the plight of codependent persons. They are now developing a full scale of programs related to codependency needs beginning with information seminars to long-term individual and group therapies. Some conversations with a respected minister who knows about such a counseling center or just calling or going to the center to inquire and investigate would be appropriate. Such centers would welcome your inquiries. They are ready to serve interested people and to talk about their programs.

Finally, check the list of self-help groups and agencies related to codependency listed in the back of this book. A letter of request or perhaps a phone call will give you the date and time of day when meetings of local chapters in your area are held. Remember, if you attend one of their meetings, do not judge the quality or the value of their codependency programs by your first impressions of people you meet in an open, public group meeting of a local chapter of a twelve-step group. The people there have been and are victims of abuse by their families, society at large, and by themselves in an attempt to escape their pain.

Listen to their stories. Listen deeply to the spiritual hunger in their lives. You may not wish to be in that kind of environment. Your own recovery plan does not have to include attending such groups, but you will be glad you did attend. When you first go, travel with a friend or group of friends. If you do not like it there, go somewhere else. Do not let a poor first impression block your resolve to get a program set up for your own personal recovery.

It may be very important for you to take the twelve-step program very seriously for yourself as a part of your recovery. You may need not only to attend the open sessions of the groups, but also to select and make a covenant with a sponsor. This sponsor is a recovering codependent who agrees to walk with you through your twelve-step process, to be available to listen, and be with you during the heavy times of living in your same old environment while making the decidedly clean personality changes you adopt while recovering. In many instances, this method of beginning work on recovery is the only one within financial reach.

Occasionally, the codependency/addiction system in your family may result in the hospitalization of the codependent as well as or instead of the addict. In such cases, you will be surprised to learn that appropriate inpatient care for codependents is becoming available in many more locations in the United States. It is still unavailable in some locales, however. Sometimes, a residential center is the best place for codependents to receive care. Codependents who are also addicts have already received good attention in several chemical dependency treatment centers in some places. The likelihood is that more such facilities will be expanded to include programs for codependents and that new facilities will become available.

In most instances, however, codependents will receive outpatient treatment in clinics, institutes, and counseling offices of a variety of professional persons for a long time to come. More and more are being seen in the context of marriage and family counseling centers. This mode of help for codependents remains the most available throughout the nation. The twelve-step groups are the most economical places to receive help with recovery programs. Group work or group therapy programs are the next most expensive and have a high rating for contribution toward successful recovery. Individual or private counseling will cost the same as other individual therapy sources in your area. Most expensive of all will be the residential care or hospital facilities. Some insurance companies will cover part of the reasonable and customary charges made here, but large parts of the cost of care will fall on the patient and the patient's family.

Whenever and wherever possible, and even in the face of great sacrifice of time and money, a codependent determined to recover is urged to select a counselor who has been properly trained to counsel with codependents and to begin work as soon as possible after making the decision to begin recovery. Check this out with your local alcohol or chemical treatment team members. For Christians, check on whether the pastoral counselor you may use is well enough prepared to work with persons who are codependent.

When selecting a counselor, check these resources: your pastor; other pastors in the area known for their counseling preparation; physicians, especially known and trusted psychiatrists; and local social workers and family counselors who should certainly be aware of those with the best training to assist codependents. For appropriate referrals, call the chaplains in any of your local hospitals and the counseling centers attached to them; call the professors of counseling disciplines in the seminaries and colleges near you; or call the nearest major agencies of your own denomination. They all have health care personnel who should know the counselors in their areas and around the country who are able to provide the best help for you in your location.

Above all, find the best-prepared person available even if you must travel several miles away from home each week and begin your stage II work as soon as possible. Stage I is often called the Survival Stage. In stage II, your recovery begins.

Second Step in Recovery

In this stage, you, a codependent person, take a good look at yourself. It is a time to test out the truth of the label, "I am a codependent." You will see yourself on that day as a person who is continuously hammered and beaten emotionally if not physically by your environment. But the most important focus for study in stage II is not on the people in your history nor the events happening around you each day. The place to look is at yourself and especially *inside* yourself.

Be prepared to discover how much you believe about yourself

is part of a daydream or fantasy and how much is factual and truthful. In your private daydreams, you may have seen yourself as quite powerful, able to control yourself and others around you from time to time. You may have fancied yourself as being pretty good, no matter what others thought.

If you were asked to give a report from your private musings at the beginning of your work with the counselor, you would probably confess that you believed you were quite able to get close to being perfect. You feel able to take care of almost any crisis that might arise, certainly more able to do things than the insensitive clods around you. Now, with the help of this therapist, you will begin to see all of this in a more realistic light. Your private fantasies will be seen for what they have been, a group of maneuvers to make yourself feel good, and all of this to counterbalance a deep feeling of very low self-worth.

Strange, but these things never really did help your self-worth at all. They just made you feel very sad inside. Now that you are looking at the things you have done and continue to do, you really begin to feel like a clod. Where did you learn to do these things? Why have you been trying to act like the family hero? Why do you feel you must always do well, make great grades, make people proud, solve people's problems, take care of weaker people, and above all pretend you never have any bad feelings or problems of your own? And why have you even started to believe your own lies?

At this time in the therapeutic look inside yourself, the codependent you begin to discover some awful things. You really have had some bad feelings. You have some memories stored from the past you can recall in "living color." No Hollywood recording can capture living color, accurate wording, or deep emotion like you can in your memory.

In the appropriate therapeutic space of your counselor's office, you become able to relive these moments, even the most terrible ones; and you are able with the caring guidance of the therapist to reinterpret them more accurately. You discover you now can make more sense out of them. You can actually get a better look at why they happened. You can now see more of your own part in the dramas. You can now reinterpret the events in ways more easily managed in the future.

Because you revisit the past in this way, you are able both to make some new decisions about today and regain some things you had lost. You now also have been able to look into the future with some hope.

Of course this does not happen quickly or easily. It takes time, it takes trust, and for the Christian, it is a deeply moving spiritual experience. These events are accomplished, as all events are for believers, in the very presence of God who honors such hard work and who blesses the process of forgiveness in the past and grace for the future.

Such a result is best accomplished with a therapist who himself or herself is a believing Christian, but that is not an absolutely necessary requirement. Any therapist who honors and respects the spirituality of a client may nurture the spiritual awareness of the presence of God and encourage the believer to make use of that power also to move toward health and recovery. God, for the Christian, is always on the side of health and recovery.

The second part of stage II is to happen at the same time as the first part. The distorted self is expelled by the codependent.

You must acknowledge that you cannot just reject the self you have become over the past twenty, thirty, or forty years in a few days or weeks. It certainly cannot happen by using the strength of your willpower alone, no matter how powerful your counselor may be. Nothing less than divine intervention is necessary. At this time, participation in a twelve-step group or at least a careful study and adoption of the twelve-step process becomes an important parallel process to the counseling.[4]

Faith in God begins, continues, and ends in the belief that God is all-powerful and has set limits on us. Accepting those limits at this time is most vital to us in our codependence. We cannot control our feelings forever. We might manage to do so in some ways and for a time; but, when we feel badly in spite of telling ourselves to feel good, our feelings usually have the best of the argument.

Even the strongest medication lasts only briefly.

If we can't control our own feelings, why do we think we can control the feelings of other people? And why do we attempt to do so? And why do we suppose we can control their thoughts and actions? God created the human spirit for freedom, not to be dominated by others. Indeed, if the human spirit is subjected to domination, it eventually will become diseased and then spread disease, or it will resurface and reclaim itself.

One of the most remarkable demonstrations of this on a large scale was made in the fall of 1989 in the eastern bloc Communist nations. Citizens long rigidly controlled by their governments began to march in the streets as an expression of their desire for freedom. In spite of being clubbed, subjected to water cannon and tear gas attacks, in spite of stern orders to leave the streets, the people had lived through enough communist control. It was time for the free spirit to speak, and no amount of threats would stop their expressions. And they would not change their minds.

The leaders tried persuasion, but no amount of persuasion would change them. The leaders tried to make concessions, and no amount of concessions would alter their resolution to be free. Thus the Communist party heads resigned in disgrace and defeat.

Codependents in stage II discover that willpower is not effective as a tool to control others. It is just as ineffective in the long term as political dictatorships like fascism, communism, and feudalism. Families dominated by codependent patriarchs or matriarchs may function briefly and may temporarily meet some real or imagined external foe; but they do immeasurable harm to family members, especially the children. In the long haul, domination and control of the human will seems to spread destruction and emotional disease.

Willpower has its proper place. That place is to be exerted only on a person's own self. Its major effectiveness with other people is at the point of testimony, not coercion. Joshua's most powerful statement to his people was a testimonial, "But as for me and my house, we will serve the Lord" (Josh. 24:15). To build a person's own best potential testimony and example are ways to achieve the highest possible kind of influence in personal and family living.

To do this, self-knowledge, ongoing self-awareness, and strategies for self-expression are vital. They are important ongoing goals in any program of recovery, and are particular targets of interest in stage II codependency therapy programs.

Third Step in Recovery

Stage III will find you, the codependent patient, beginning the massively difficult task of discovering the core issues of your relationship dysfunction. You must ask yourself:

- What are my symptoms?
- Can I make a list of them?
- Can I face telling myself, God, and my counselor about each of my symptoms?

This part of the process is similar to the spiritual exercise of confession. Yes, you say, I do these things. And I did it to this person and to that person. As you do this, you are uncovering and admitting your sins. You seek first to receive forgiveness from God and from others, and secondly to find a way to forgive those who have sinned against you.

A word here needs to be spoken about the Christian process of forgiveness, the most spiritually vital part of the codependency recovery process for the Christian. The giving of forgiveness, for Christians, is a matter of surrendering to God any right to let offenses committed unto them by others turn into hardness of heart or grudges. More positively, it is a matter of coming to the level of spiritual maturity where you can pray as Jesus did for forgiveness even for those who crucified Him. This makes it possible to understand Jesus' teaching, "For if you forgive others their trespasses, God will also forgive you; but if you do not forgive others their trespasses, neither will God forgive you your trespasses."[5] Carrying a grudge causes you to make an idol of that grudge and to develop a whole system of behaviors around that grudge. Such activity is neither healthy nor spiritual. Recovery requires the surrendering of your grudges to God.

When you are able to forgive others freely, however, you have become mature enough to make some major decisions. Continued recovery may bring you to difficult decisions about how you will communicate, where you will live, with whom you will live, and how you will invest your vocational time. You may quite well make major changes. Whatever you decide, you will relate directly, honestly, and forthrightly, and in a clean and open spirit, not in a cankered, hard-hearted way.

The more difficult task in forgiveness is the process of self-forgiveness. As a codependent you are able to give more easily than you receive. But your resistance is at its highest when it comes to receiving forgiveness. Besides, if you confess and receive forgiveness, you will become free of the load of guilt you carry. Shame will melt away. You may not believe it, but it will be true. You will have to learn a new way of life. In all tenderness I tell you that is difficult work, but well worth the effort.

Then, address your other issues. Are you a compulsive rescuer? What are some recent examples of this kind of behavior? What were some of the big ones in the past? What gets you into this compulsive behavior? What do you hope to accomplish by it? Who from your past are you trying to imitate, if anyone?

Do you communicate clearly? Or, do you find yourself blaming, begging, coercing, bribing, advising, talking much and saying little, guarding what you say in order to please certain people and not to offend others? Do you overreact to things that happen? Do you spend time trying to catch people not doing what they are supposed to do? Do you really believe good things will never happen to you? Do you often feel like a victim, even in little things? Do you habitually not trust yourself, your feelings, your decisions, other people, and even wonder if God has abandoned you?

Do you do more than your share in every relationship, such as in marriage? Do you do more around the house than your partner? Do you provide sexual affection on your partner's schedule but never ask for yourself? Do you insist on paying more when three couples go together to have a pizza supper brought in to your house, even though you furnish the drinks and other snacks for the evening? Do you sometimes feel so angry you want to be completely irresponsible, but you wind up being even more responsible than ever? Do you sometimes laugh when you want to cry? Do you lie and cover up things, even when it is not a national emergency?

This is the stage in which you discover your own personal core issues. You may begin with the behaviors, but you will move back to the roots, and finally to the spiritual depths of your person to seek healing for your codependent pattern as it relates to this core issue. You may remain in individual counseling with your therapist, or you may move into a group setting with other recovering codependent persons and see your therapist individually only once a month or every six weeks.

This group will be quite a challenge for you. But you will be surprised how well the members will understand you and be able to share things that are useful to you. You, in turn, will be able to share in ways that will be useful to them. In the community of the group you will be able to design and then put into practice new strategies for replacing the old, unsuccessful codependent patterns you have begun to leave behind. The group will help you. They will serve as an arena for you to test your new models for communication. They will feed back information as to whether you are following your plan. They will catch every slip backward into your old codependent patterns. One or more of them may become good and lifelong friends.

Your counselor will be able to advise you before you begin as to whether you are ready to join a group or not. Your counselor may be one of the leaders of the group you join. You should make the final choice yourself. Joining or not joining may be a test of your growing openness, a test of your growing strength, or a test of your resolve to do the things you have planned in one-to-one therapy.

The group leader or leaders should be skilled in the arts of working with family and group systems, and they should also have some special training in working with recovering codependents and chemical dependents. They should have had sufficient personal, therapeutic attention that they themselves are recovering well, and they should have consultation available.

An important mark of stage III is the growing ability to see people in your relationships with an extra pair of eyes. You see yourself relating comfortably with others for the first time; you begin to see how others are relating to you and you enjoy them as people; and you realize you can see everyone around you as a part of the whole conversation. You see more and you are thrilled with what you see and are more intimately involved with every relationship.

But, the most important part of stage III is to get ready for part IV. Actually, part III blends into part IV so there is a hazy line, or a fine line, between them. In part IV, you are becoming stronger. Your are consistently reclaiming yourself and affirming your new selfhood. You have continued to be surrendered to God but empowered to life and to other people. You are ready to leave therapy.

Fourth Step in Recovery

This is the final stage of your therapy before you launch into your continued recovery process on your own. Your recent sessions with your counselor may have been spaced out on a schedule of an appointment every two weeks, then once a month for about four or six months during the end of stage III and into stage IV. The time of counseling is drawing to a close.

There will be some joy here.

Wow!

You have completed this part of the program and now you have grown spiritually, emotionally, intellectually, and in so many ways you can scarcely imagine. You will be glad to have the trips to the counselor's office over; and the money can be put to use in a lot of other places.

But you are starting to be a little nervous too.

No more regular support from your counselor.

You have moved away from being a relationship addict in your old life. Now you are facing the challenge of moving away from a healthy relationship with the counselor. If you are like most people, you have become dependent upon the counselor to some degree in spite of the counselor's skill in setting people free.

Now it's time for you to step out on your own.

Your counselor has set the plan. You may come in for a checkup in four months. You may even make an appointment now if you wish.

Of course you will make the appointment immediately.

But the therapy phase is over.

Review of the Counseling

In the last counseling sessions, you have performed a solid review of the therapy. You are sure you have done at least five things and you can say with joy:

- I have turned denial that I was codependent into the affirmation, "I was, and I am a codependent; but I am a recovering codependent";
- I have turned my strategies of defeat (the old ways) into occasions of surrender and spiritual confession to God and found help;
- I have turned my desire for control into willing spiritual acceptance of God and others;
- I have left the cave of self-pity into which I had driven myself;
- I have accepted the personal power given by God to me in creation and through my ongoing spiritual faith.

Continuing to Recover

Recovery is a lifelong process. In order for you to continue a satisfying process well begun, after completing therapy you may want to be involved in a variety of activities. First, of course, you will continue to follow with care the plan of recovery you worked out under the direction of your counselor. Periodic checkups two to four times the first year and once or twice each following year would be one way you could keep up that contact and renew the benefit of your investment in therapy.

Cultivating social relationships with a small group of recovering friends, seeking out healthy relationships with people in church, civic, school, or other public group activities would keep you healthy and practicing your recovery. Continuation in a twelve-step program on a weekly basis or as needed for a boost if other recovering persons are not available for relationships would be a good idea.

It would be important too for you to check with your therapist prior to your becoming a sponsor for someone else in a twelve-step program. That would be a good thing to do, but it is a situation of great temptation for a codependent. Sponsorship is obviously designed to be a health-giving relationship, but it may deteriorate into a codependent rescue operation unless a recovering codependent is quite careful. At least consultation with a group of alert, recovering codependents would be an asset to you in terms of keeping you recovering and not rescuing.

Work using your appropriate strengths in nurturing, teaching, and organizing/directing (in moderation) for your church, PTA, or other organization are examples of creative outlets for your appropriate helping energies. Again, have some people who know you to serve as your resource people. They should be people to whom you can talk openly about the process of what is going on and who will keep an open covenant with you to assist you to keep on recovering.

Finally, you might want to find a way to encourage your church or local group to sponsor space for twelve-step programs. Sometimes groups needing to be formed are never organized for lack of appropriate meeting space while churches or club buildings go unused. Your encouragement may be the difference between a group getting space and helping many people or not. Remember, the church or local group may say no. They may be afraid; they may have bad stereotypes of twelve-step programs; or they may for other reasons not want the building to be used by outside groups. A mark of recovery is to be able to take a definite no without taking it personally, without overreacting, and with an appropriate spirit of recovery.

Notes

1. The basic outline for the stages of treatment for codependent persons is taken from Timmen Cermak, *Diagnosing and Treating Co-Dependence: A Guide For Professionals With Chemical Dependents, their Spouses, and Children* (Minneapolis, Minn.: Johnson Institute Books, 1986), 61-93.

2. Wayne E. Oates, *On Becoming Children of God,* (Philadelphia: Westminster Press, 1970), chapter 9 im passim.

3. John Friel and Linda Friel, *Adult Children: The Secrets of Dysfunctional Families* (Deerfield Beach, Fla.: Health Communications, Inc., 1988), 171-72.

4. See chapter 1, page 39.

5. Matthew 6:14-15. This capsule teaching from the Sermon on the Mount has some flavor of a new legalism, but this is softened in so many other places as Jesus applied it to actual situations. In spite of the textual difficulties, the application of the forgiveness principle in the first section of John 8 is an example. Christians are not to be *stone throwers,* nor are they to be *stone carriers.* Their task is to work out a way in their own settings (families, neighborhoods, institutions, cultures, etc.) to be forgivers and to become ministers of forgiveness and reconciliation. The sad part of the John 8 story for me is the answer to the question, Woman, where are your accusers? The people most needing forgiveness had already left the scene. Jesus had forgiveness for law breakers like the adulteress; and He also had forgiveness for compulsive law makers and abusive law enforcers as they came into spiritual relationship to God. And He also had messages about recovery, such as, "Go, and sin no more" (John 8:11, KJV).

5

Does Codependency Affect the Churches?

So far, we have seen that codependency is a process that affects individual persons, persons who are in a love or a family relationship with an addict of one variety or another. They are persons who have grown up in a variety of places in the midst of many different kinds of dysfunctional relationship patterns.

We have seen that codependency is present in some fashion in many relationships between two people, especially married couples; it is seen in families, both in families living under the same roof and extended families living close to or distant from each other; and we can now project it to take place within groups of people who gather together regularly for a variety of purposes.

Because codependence is so prevalent in our culture, traces of codependency most likely can be found in all human activities where groups of people live, work, or play together. This is true whether the group is as small as two persons or as large as many thousands. This may be true in the smallest group of three or four gathered regularly for any purpose, or where states or nations organize to conduct business for the good of the people.

Because that is true, codependency as it is currently defined is certainly to be found in the church. If we look carefully, we will be able to see it there. It is my experience that when you learn the methods of codependence, even the most casual glance at most churches will reveal the presence of codependent behavior. Most probably, you will be able to see it in the following places.

Individual Codependents Among the Members

First, you will see codependence in the local church in the way individuals who have developed mild, strong, or compulsive needs to help others act in the churches. They will crash into projects to help whether or not they are invited. Whether it is their strong need to control their environment in order to feel comfort, or whether they are really unable to recognize boundaries between themselves and others, they butt in in the strongest ways. They may cover their activities by insisting they are doing the Lord's work or just trying to make things more perfect, the way Jesus would want them to be done, but they will be at the forefront controlling.

Others will help from the sidelines with their suggestions. They will imply that we should be ashamed for the church to do less than this, or it would be awful for us not to do better than last year. They will offer to sacrifice themselves in order to be examples for others. Then they will proceed to overpower any opposition by nurturing whatever guilt they can find in competitors. They will use fear or shame to motivate their newfound slaves to get things activated and moving. Some pastors and other ministers, as well as laypersons, have been known to use these methods of motivation.

Then there are those individuals who protect the people who don't do what they promise to do. They make excuses for them, build a web of stories to protect them from confrontation by others. In many ways they interfere with a clear and open communication among the membership. These people are often balanced by their opposites, codependents who overreact to everything. Overreactors fly off the handle, whether raising a storm over a small need or a great one, a minor infraction or a major sin. Occasionally, the overreactors and the protectors become antagonists and create a climate of dis-ease in the congregation. The overreactors cry out against someone or some change in the regular way of doing things, and the rescuers/protectors mount a crusade to fend off such attacks. Churches with opposite codepen-

dent types like this seldom have quiet business meetings for longer than a few months. Is it any wonder the whole church family is
desperate to keep things quiet and not rock the boat?

The worst kind of codependent to inflict the church is the person who has great ideas, who can plan and sell those ideas to
others easily, but who just cannot seem to follow the project
through to the end. After beginning a project, the codependent is
out of town on business or has some convenient emergency taking up the time. The program may become a total failure. Then, if
you are the codependent member who started the whole thing,
you may be so hard on yourself that you will consider leaving the
church, or at least fade into the background and become nearly
inactive.

Two kinds of codependent activity are then kicked into gear.
First, one or more persons with rescue patterns will try to restore
you to fellowship by giving you much attention and exaggerated,
if not false, praise. Even though you know many people in the
church do not share the same feelings, you love the attention and
may be seduced to return, to repeat the pattern again as soon as
you regain strength and others trust you again. You may even
trick yourself into believing you are atoning for your past crimes
by your newest perfect-to-be plan. But you will withdraw again.
That is your pattern. You are addicted to it.

These churches are filled with an enormous number of unfinished projects and disappointed members. This is especially tragic when the unfinished projects brought unexplainable disappointment to young persons and children whose reservoir of
trustworthy persons and events was damaged by the loss of hope
related to these aborted projects.

A second kind of response to an unfinished project is furnished
by resourceful rescuers or by normally healthy people who are
alert and competent enough to finish the project when you have
left the unfinished mess. Then much can be salvaged. However,
the rescuer may come just a little bit closer to burnout, the condition that usually sidelines a codependent and others in leadership
or heavy-duty serving positions in the churches.

A troublesome kind of codependent is the adult child of an alcoholic who lies when it would be just as easy to tell the truth. Rarely do these people just openly lie in a way that can be seen by everyone immediately. Usually, the lies are little, inconsequential, fibs. However, the lies keep alive the low self-esteem of the codependent members, keep their guilt level quite high, and add to the tank full of shame they carry around with them. Adult children of alcoholics are so used to having to lie to get by, the habit continues to eat away at their inner selves and blocks any true move toward deeper spiritual growth. These codependents are unreliable models for other Christians, as well as being a menace to themselves. Such persons require some open, frank, and honest love of themselves as persons in concert with some direct confrontation against the lies.

Recently, I attended a worship service that was wonderfully prepared in advance by the pastor and staff. The music, the prayers, the Scripture, the sermon were all designed to focus on Jesus as the Truth of God. The pastor admonished and exhorted his listeners to give a good witness to such a God by living lives of truth and honesty. Lies were not to cross the lips of Christians.

But there was a small glitch that morning. It came in an impromptu comment by the pastor during the announcement period just before the formal worship service began. He told us the minister of music had recovered from recent back trouble and was able to lead music in the service that morning. The congregation gave warm support with polite applause. However, the pastor requested that the congregation not tell the minister of music's spouse, who was away from home on business that Sunday, that the cane the doctor required the minister of music to use that day had intentionally been left in the minister of music's office. The congregation was then given a pastoral indulgence to tell a little white lie if necessary to cover the truth. They were not to tell the spouse or the doctor that the minister of music disobeyed medical orders.

We never know when our codependence will break through our most carefully manufactured veneers. It sneaks up on us as we relate in the church as well as when we relate at home.

Married Couple Codependents Among the Members

A second place codependence is seen in the church is in the relationships (with all of their codependent dimensions) married people bring to church with them when they come.

Of special note is the couple who were both reared in strict rule-keeping families and who operate their own family in the same way. In their strictly disciplined way, they are both deeply committed workaholics. They have no children. Their rigidity shows up in almost every phase of their lives, both together and in the church. Apparently, they do not have any personal interest in or time for leisure. They cannot or will not play, and they seemingly have no humor or happiness in their lives. Everything is so deadly serious. They oppose mission trips for the young people. That's too much like playing instead of really working for the Lord. They oppose spending church funds for social events for singles, and they barely tolerate Sunday School picnics and stewardship banquets because people seem to want to have fun instead of to serve God.

Families whose members are composed of one or more adult children of alcoholic parents frequently bring interesting dynamics to any church. This is especially true if the ACA is in a leadership position or a staff minister. Of the thirteen primary characteristics of ACAs identified, at least six are extremely relevant to the church. The first one relates to ACAs not knowing what normal is. Not having a routine set of procedures for the development of the church programs is often seen in smaller churches. Living without planning ahead is the way ACAs usually function. Suddenly, Christmas, Easter, graduation, the pastor's or church's anniversary, or some other event needing special recognition seems to appear before thought to prepare is made. Hastily thrown together and somewhat chaotic programs are often presented to the disappointment of many and the exasperation or exhaustion of the few. ACAs pay such happenings no mind because chaos is the briar patch in which they were reared. Soon, many non-ACA members are leaving the church because they cannot tolerate this sloppy way of doing God's work.

Difficulties are also presented when leaders make plans for special events. When things are scheduled but are done in radically different ways each time they are presented, trouble brews. People who prefer tradition, who like things to be done the same way year after year, are usually very upset when nothing is the same. "It's Christmas, and the shepherds wear bathrobes and the angels wear wings." No matter how well or how artistically things may be done, if they do not settle into a recognizable tradition, many regular members are unsettled. ACAs often become bored with tradition.

Church members often use codependent strategies to relate to addicts within the church family, regardless of the addiction or the person addicted. This is especially true of persons who are suspected, accused, or found to be guilty of some addictive behavior that is considered deviant by society, such as certain law breaking or abusive behaviors. Chief among these addictive behaviors are drunken driving, gambling, child abuse, sexual abuse, and physical abuse of several kinds. Many of the codependent roles appear in the ways church people respond to addicts. Most of the membership may usually be counted on to be persecutors. A smaller, but equally vocal, group plays the role of rescuer. The rest of the folk usually remain neutral.

Codependence and the Pastor

It is of special importance to notice the flavor of the relationship between the chief minister—the pastor—and the congregation. Special treatment has long been afforded the pastor. While it is vital to make a clear distinction between the normal and expected behavior that may pass under the category of human frailty, it is not normal for the congregation to react in less than honest and forthright ways to a pastor who does not behave as a called minister of the gospel.

It is important to notice that congregations as well as individuals may behave in codependent ways. Frequently, a congregation may behave as a codependent context for a minister who has developed a minor or even a more serious addiction. When this happens, the minister may continue for long periods of time in the addiction without being challenged in any way.

At other times, churches may relate in normal and healthy ways to a minister's addictions. They may confront them in such a way as to bring the minister to the point of regaining his spiritual center, a recommitment of life to Christ, and to the beginning of a lifelong process of recovery. If you were the minister and you exhibited addictive or codependent characteristics, it would be an act of kindness to you as well as a service to God's work for you to be challenged to secure the kind of assistance that would restore you to your full spiritual ability to serve the Lord.

A more difficult scenario relates to the minister who is normal and healthy and is confronted within the church by large numbers of codependent individuals and families of addicts and their codependent relatives. Having been there for years, these families have established a routine set of codependent habits, rituals, and methodologies within the church. Seeking a spiritual center for the church as a community and seeking to bring Christ to a place of leadership in such a church is a tremendous task. To write about this would take a separate volume of this size, so I merely mention it here and will illustrate it briefly later in the chapter.

First, however, I address the issue of ministerial addiction and congregational codependence. The most casual evaluation of the relationship between pastors and churches points out the usual generosity of the laypersons toward their pastors in whom they have confidence and whom they have grown to love. While there are obvious exceptions the pastor is offered tender and gentle handling by most church memberships.

I speak mainly of pastors who are reasonably well and are able to give full attention to church work, who do give their best efforts to the tasks of leading worship and preaching, of pastoral care and visitation of the sick or infirm, and to the routine administrative and educational needs of the church. These pastors are often paid well, and they have reasonable fringe benefit packages.

Many ministers have other benefits ordinary church members do not have. Many are invited to participate in the leadership activities of communities. Some are routinely invited to sit on boards and trusteeships. Ministers are often invited into homes for meals; and they are inundated by gifts of food, clothing, other goods, money from individuals, and favors such as the use of recreational equipment and vacation lodges.

And when they get in trouble, they frequently have the charges overlooked. In some places in the South, the discount policy for ministers is still in place from physicians, dentists, and other practitioners. As my colleague Wayne Oates has said on more than one occasion, "Southern Baptist ministers are spoiled, pampered, and mollycoddled like no other group of clergy I know about in the country."

In addition to all of that, pastors, and in some cases other staff members, have long been protected from the petty incompetencies related to their tasks due to the reverence church members have for their positions. Promises made to church members in the line of duty as minister and then forgotten are often overlooked because the minister is considered to be just too busy to tend to everything.

Occasionally, some church members react in the opposite manner and express extreme hostility toward their ministers. Some make the minister's broken promises to be their celebrated cause for opposing anything the minister wants to do in the congregation. Some even agitate, silently at first and then with great energy when they develop a following, to require the minister to leave the congregation. Such overreaction is usually discounted by the congregation where the minister is otherwise doing a competent job. In such cases, the disgruntled layperson is frequently isolated with a few like-minded companions, or he or she is actually pressured to leave the church by the majority of members still loyal to the pastor. In cases where the pastor has allowed his field of relationships to become cluttered with such oversights, however, the opposition wins the day, and the minister finds himself out on his ear looking for another church, pronto.

It is also true that some gross misconduct is occasionally and even routinely covered up by a congregation. Sometimes a church, especially a fashionable First Church or at least its leading members, lead the way to protect the minister, to cover up his messes, to rescue the minister in a codependent fashion. They announce the reasons for doing this to be in order to preserve the integrity and reputation of the church. On closer investigation, their motives seem to match the motives of codependent partners of addicts.

Some examples are easy to discover. I invite you read the following stories and apply the characteristics of codependency you have learned as you have read this book.

These stories are true. The first one is a composite story using features from more than one person, and the names and places have been changed to provide anonymity for the ministers and congregations involved.

As you read these case studies, keep these questions in mind and give your own answers to them. (1) How would your church respond in these situations? (2) What advice would you give to these people and to the church? (3) In what way was codependency active on the part of the individual and the church?

A Spending Addiction

Reverend Marsh has some unusual habits related to the way he spends his money. Early in the pastorate, he purchased an expensive luxury automobile, and then he traded for a new model every year. That seemed to be beyond his financial means, but members dealt with their feelings by some good-natured teasing. He still made hospital visits and house calls in his six-year-old car, but he used the elegant sedan for Sundays, funerals, weddings, and trips out of town.

He dressed nicely, both formally and casually. He wore the finest and most expensive garments and accessories. His shoes cost more than the suits worn by most of the men in the church. Reverend Marsh was actually paid well. The church had seen a 50 percent increase in its annual baptisms since he had arrived, and had increased his salary generously each year. But his salary was still not enough to support his expensive taste in clothes and cars. This is not to mention his habit of expensive luncheons and dinners in nearby cities, his hobbies in photography and electronics, or his other lavish ways.

One evening, Larry T., the chairman of deacons of Reverend Marsh's church, received a visit from Bob S., a good friend and elder in another church in the community. Bob was also vice-president of the local Farmers and Merchant's Bank.

It was an awkward conversation for them both. The first ten minutes of small talk was obviously not the reason for the visit. Bob wished he didn't have to share his bad news, but he had promised his Methodist and Presbyterian merchant friends during the four-hour session after the Rotary Club meeting that he would tell the truth about Pastor Marsh to his deacon friend.

Marsh was in terrible financial shape. The merchants in the community had given him a 20 percent discount as a routine courtesy. When Bob S. told the merchants he was still in great difficulty, they had begun secretly to bill the pastor for only 10 percent over cost for all of his purchases, again out of courtesy to a minister and to their friends in Marsh's church. Bob urged Larry to talk with his pastor to try to clear up the problem and prevent a scandal. Larry thanked Bob for his frankness and said he would take care of it immediately.

Larry arranged a conference with his pastor the next morning. Surprisingly, the pastor seemed eager to talk about it. Even with favored treatment from the merchants, he was still falling farther behind. His short-term credit card debt in the three local banks and two national chain stores was over $27,000.00 for local purchases. In addition, he was three months behind in his home mortgage payment. The house was steadily losing market value. The pastor said he had repeatedly tried to get consolidation loans, but to no avail. No one would lend him any more money.

Larry was stunned. He had not known. The only merchants the

pastor traded with in his own church had given gifts of clothing and merchandise to the pastor. They had never charged him for anything. He apparently had taken his credit business elsewhere in town to conceal his activities.

What must be done?

Larry called a secret meeting (without the pastor) of the well-to-do members of the board of deacons. This resulted in a second meeting three days later with other members, including several of the more affluent, longtime members of the church. They all reacted the same way. They were ashamed and embarrassed.

They passed the hat right then and came up with $3,500.00 cash on the spot to begin a fund to bail the minister out. They agreed on a plan that included an ultimatum to the pastor. Mr. Jones, an older statesman and inactive deacon of the church, would be the spokesperson for the group.

The meeting was held the following Sunday evening in the pastor's study after the evening service.

The pastor had no explanation other than that he had had trouble like this all his life. He always was able to squeak by and eventually get out of the hole, but now he offered no plan, no remorse, no offer to change. He said God had called him to preach and to win souls. He just didn't bother with finances.

So the group made their offer.

They offered to pay off all his debts—every dime of them—but not to do so until the day after the moving van carried him and his family to another church field.

He agreed, and readily! They were relieved. They quickly and without thinking agreed with his conditions that they tell no one and that they give him good references, including credit references, when he left.

Don't worry, they said. They were too embarrassed to let anyone know their pastor would behave in such a manner. They were so pleased he had accepted their offer that they scarcely noticed the ease with which he did so. They were interested only in saving the reputation of the church and showing their friends in town that they could take care of their own problems.

They didn't take notice of the pastor's lack of remorse. It didn't seem to bother them that he assumed no responsibility for what he had done. And Reverend Marsh didn't even have a simple, "I'm sorry." It was almost as if he expected them to take care of him.

They secretly hoped he had learned his lesson, but they had no way of knowing whether he had or not. They really didn't care about that, if only he would go away from their town without embarrassing them any more.

He did receive a call to another place. It was to a bigger church and for a larger salary; and to the delight of the church leaders, it was more than three hundred miles away and in another state.

And he left within ten weeks.

Then the group of men paid off his debts with their own money. They cared for his house until it was sold. Then they sent him a check for the equity remaining after the sale, and they never received so much as a thank-you.

Reverend Marsh had not received any help for his addiction to spending. He had not been challenged concerning his irresponsibility.

So, as a result, he did about the same thing all over again in the next church.

The deacons of his new church were mystified that a person with such poor economic habits could have arrived in town with no debts and such good credit references.

The bankers and merchants in his new city confronted him as soon as he overextended his credit the first time. When the church people learned about his trouble, they loved him but did not coddle him.

Instead, they assisted him to get therapeutic help, but he refused to see the counselor after the second session—even though the church was paying for his care.

Reverend March is now selling insurance. He has already taken the bankruptcy law once and is approaching his second need for such relief. What a pity that a man of God should be in such need of help and have his problems swept under the rug so long that in the long run he was unable to be restored.

A Sexual Addiction

Then there was Brother Younger, a new seminary graduate who became the associate pastor of a church whose pastor was nearing retirement. Brother Younger was outwardly competent in almost all ministerial skills, especially for a man so young. And he was strikingly handsome.

Although he was engaged to be married to a lovely young woman who was a graduate student in a distant city, many young women in his new church set their caps for him. Many of their mothers saw him to be a good catch and openly entered into competition with each other to see if one of them could assist one of their own daughters to become Mrs. Younger.

The situation was too much temptation for this young man. He tells the story that he kept company with two or three of these lovely young daughters of the church. And his sexual addiction was reactivated. He had picked up the habit in high school, but he had successfully put it aside as a result of his rededication of faith in Christ and as a part of his answer to a call from God to study for the ministry.

He told this story along with memories of scores of brief liaisons and longer affairs with other women. And this after being celibate in college and seminary, after winning the girl of his dreams whom he did marry and who stayed with him even after she learned the truth. They had been married twenty-two years, were parents of three beautiful children, and all the while these sexual affairs had been going on. He had been serving as staff member or pastor of six churches, and he had been secretly living out a life of sexual addiction.

The church in which his addiction was discovered tenderly offered to give him a one-year sabbatical leave for medical treatment and recovery with the option to return as pastor if he could get the recommendation of his medical team to support it. He decided not to accept the offer of continued employment before he entered therapy. But he accepted the forgiveness and love of this understanding group of believers whose faith in his potential recovery and steadfast faithfulness since that time was apparently an important factor both in his present health and his present profession to which he contributes meaningfully.

An Administrative Style Addiction

Then there was the pastor of a church whose membership was made up mostly of families whose breadwinners worked in factories on assembly lines. He had grown up in just such a church. The pastor's father had been an alcoholic. Although he never read the list of thirteen characteristics of adult children of alcoholics, several prominent ones fit his life-style to a *t*.

There had never been a set of guidelines for almost anything in the church before he became pastor. It had grown to nearly four hundred members just before he arrived, and now it was nearing six hundred. He enjoyed making up the rules as he went along, but the administrative tasks were really getting on his nerves. He did stewardship emphases occasionally, but in spite of increasing membership, there never seemed to be enough money to call a minister of education. They almost never had teachers for every Sunday School need; only the women's mission organization seemed to be well staffed. He went from crisis to crisis, but that seemed like the church in which he grew up, so he did not worry. The problems mounted up, little ones, and he thought that was somehow his fault so he would just have to try harder. And he did try harder, nearly eighty hours each week.

Thus he collapsed on the softball field with his first heart attack. The interim pastor was a newly retired minister who was not an adult child of an alcoholic. He attempted to organize the chaos into some general pattern. He established a nominating committee, a stewardship committee, and focused the deacons toward a family ministry program.

The church reconsidered within three months and let the interim pastor go; then they called another person as permanent associate pastor. This man was an adult child of an alcoholic. He was used to handling things on a crisis basis. He didn't want to organize anything. He preferred church to be much like the chaotic and disorganized place the church remembered things being. And they welcomed their pastor back with love and affection.

A Challenge for Church Members

Perhaps your church has no evidences of codependent behavior. No individual members of your church, no family groups within your church, nor does the church family itself function with any codependent patterns or characteristics.

I congratulate you.

However, I challenge you to begin to observe your church and perhaps to discover some members who do exhibit codependent characteristics. Pray for them. Be friends to them. Make a covenant with God and ask for an opportunity to testify to the joy that has come to you now that you are recovering. Perhaps you will challenge others to begin the pilgrimage of recovery as well.

6

So Where Is Codependency Now?

How Does Codependence Help Us to Think About Life?

Codependency is an idea whose time has come. It helps us to understand ourselves more clearly, and it has given us a way to look at our methods of dealing with each other. It has pointed out some reasons for our day-to-day pains. Codependency provides a way for us to discover why some of us have grown up to feel worthless, useless, and without much hope in spite of much promise to be otherwise.

The codependency model has shown us again how resilient the human spirit really is. When placed in a subservient role, the human spirit may go underground for a while, but in time it rebels against its captivity and discovers a partial if not total way to defeat its most relentless captors. When you are codependent, you might be down, but you will find a way to hang tough and to exercise control again, even if it is in a devious manner. The entire codependency system shows that human beings can find and develop many clever ways to fight back. It shows that people have been able to dominate others, even from a lower position, and to become commanders while still wearing the uniforms of ordinary sailors.

Codependence has helped us to sort out the difference between the kinds of loving, caring, and self-giving that are voluntary and the kinds that are involuntary. It helps us to appreciate the result of aggressive action, even those actions filled with evil intent. It has helped us to see that our families really are impor-

151

tant. Codependency has reminded us, among other things, that our families pass on not only physical characteristics but also many habits, styles of relationship, and entire patterns of relating to other people, groups, institutions, and the whole world. Family living is never to be ignored or taken for granted. The ways we live together and especially the ways we attend to the tasks of child rearing are to be measured and intentional.

Codependence has helped us to see that human beings are not just gently inclined toward winning. It has helped us to see that human beings are driven toward life-styles of domination. Even those people who live lives of self-sacrifice find a way to call public attention to their sacrifices and to carve out a small arena where they can be victorious, powerful, and winners.

Above all, codependence has shown decisively that in one way or another, all humans are addicts. And, as inescapable addicts, we function mostly in ways to avoid pain. In as many ways as we are able, we avoid pain. We would rather become involved with some kind of substance than to face reality with its pain. That sounds illogical, but that is the way we act. We would rather become addicted to another person and meeting that person's needs or to some process to occupy our time and take our minds and feelings away from present reality with the kinds of pain that reality may give us.

We are creative in hiding from ourselves the fact that we become addicted, but we seem not to notice we are becoming addicted only so long as we still have personal strength to resist. After we discover we are hooked, we cannot escape of our own free wills.

If we escape from substance abuse, that is, if we avoid alcohol, illegal drugs, cigarettes, and even coffee, chocolate, or other foods, we will find a way to become addicted to some process like gambling, shopping, spending, or physical or emotional cruelty. If these addictions fail to capture us and we begin to face our own existence, we are seduced into looking at other people's reality and spending our time and energies solving their problems. We slip into relationship addictions; we become codependent.

And we are all hopelessly involved in addictions. We all practice one or another of them. And we are all permanently changed by our addictions.

If we stay with any one of them, we will be destroyed by them. And we will be destroyed before attempting to come to grips with ourselves, the meaning of life, and before attempting to make decisions or commitments about the ways in which we want to invest our time, energies, and affections. The bottom line of the entire addiction/codependence process is that we are forever deflected from our own best selves as humans. And that, above all, means that we are deflected from developing our own personhood and our own internal best selves.

The main outcome of the codependence studies, then, is to bring us to the point of challenge about the meaning of life. It forces us to acknowledge our conscious or unconscious choices to be addicts rather than free, healthy, contributing persons. It illustrates with accuracy our human inability to escape or in any way to free ourselves from the clutches of the debilitating forces of addiction.

In order to become free, to begin to recover, and to remain open to a chosen path of recovery, something else is needed. Perhaps the best lesson of codependence is that we cannot be rescued by someone else. Such a rescue would defeat us. It would prove how worthless, powerless, and useless we really are. We are the only ones able to help ourselves. So the only help for us is beyond us and within us.

The only direction at the end of pointers like that is a spiritual one. So then, codependence teaches us that spirituality is the only place to begin to find healing and recovery for addiction.

Nearly fifty years of successful twelve-step programs demonstrates how people can find the answer to their dilemmas only if they activate their own spirituality, if they make connection with the Spirit of God who awaits such an approach from every person. This is not only true of the alcoholics and other known substance abusers, it is becoming very clear that it is especially true of the addiction that has come to be known as codependence.

Again, codependence teaches us that spirituality is the only source of help for persons who are addicted!

Now we are left to discover spirituality.

How Does Codependence Help Us Think About Christianity?

Codependence has enabled us to take a fresh look at the Christian faith. When Christianity is practiced as the Bible teaches it and when it is taught as Jesus Christ taught and practiced it during the brief period of His earthly life, Christianity is intensely spiritual. It begins, continues on a daily basis, and extends into the future as a spiritual religion.

Actually, there are many thoughts, ideas, teachings, practices, rituals, customs, traditions, methods, and interpretations of the Christian faith alive and well today. The churches and groups where they are practiced are the places you have available to discover Christianity today. If you were to choose a particular group of Christians with whom to share your life of faith, you would see how that particular group interprets and practices the faith.

However, you may miss spirituality in the midst of churchianity. Therefore, you need to begin with a personal experience with God. This experience should continue with the study of God's Word, prayer, and personal spiritual growth. True Christian spirituality will put you on a journey away from codependence. As you journey away from codependence, you may want to participate in the church's customs and practices that grow out of the basic spiritual foundations of the faith.

Now you must choose! What kind of spirituality will be yours?

Many addicts have been encouraged to move toward a spiritual solution to their addiction and have great trouble. They have followed a sponsor's advice and have chosen a God-as-you-understand-God kind of spirituality. That, of course, is better than no spirituality at all. But it just throws you on the mercy of your past memories and experiences. It requires you to select what is spiritual by a process of accepting or rejecting those memories of religious faith you have accumulated from your background.

Or, you may, in a continuously codependent attitude, submit

yourself to the whims and prejudices of people you know, even your sponsor, and swap your addiction/codependency for straightforward dependency. Remember, people who may be quite expert in a lot of other areas of life are not necessarily competent in religion also. Besides, if you wish a personal spirituality, you must seek your own and not accept one from someone else. It will only be a substitute spirituality. Be especially alert not to move into a spirituality that is cold and distant, magical, under your own control, or otherwise codependent. That's a tough assignment, but that's how reality is. A true personal spirituality is not for softhearted or weak-kneed souls.

While you are taking charge of your own life, I recommend you take charge of your own spirituality as well. Seek a spirituality based on the needs and satisfactions of your recovering self.

What do I say about spirituality? Taking my own advice to do as I have recommended here in this book, my general testimony is recorded here. Chapter 3 is a cognitive outline of that faith. The next brief paragraphs are a more direct witness.

For me, spirituality has been and continues to be in the context of the Christian faith. In Christ, I have met God as a God of grace, One who accepts me as I am, receives my confessions with loving forgiveness in Christ, and who offers daily blessing to me as a desired child in God's own family.

I formerly tried to control my life, and whenever I attempt that again, I still fail miserably. Sensing that failure, I also sense the grace-bearing Spirit of God calling my spirit to the spiritual place of meeting. His Spirit calls me to renew my covenant, to reaffirm my joy as God's child, and to surrender as much more of myself to Christ as I possibly can do. I continually sense in my spirit the invitation of God to surrender those less godly parts of myself—without becoming a slave—and to gain new strength as a continuously developing Christian.

The gentleness of these words masks the difficulty of the road, the harshness of the battles with sin and a variety of addictions, and the anguish of spirit, emotion, and mind that have all been such a real part of my journey of faith. But the trip has been well worth it. Now the only difficulty is having to learn with each passing month some other major process or activity to surrender to God and to work into my own plan of recovery.

For you, my reader, I wish the discovery of a rewarding personal, autonomous spirituality. God wants you to be forgiven. In Christ, God has already provided for your forgiveness. God is open to a relationship with you. I hope you can allow your spiritual capacity to be open to a relationship with God. If you choose a Christian to begin conversations about this, pray that God will lead you to a truly Spirit-filled believer who will lead you to an open, autonomous faith in God through Christ.

For those of you already Christian, you have become painfully aware that you are addicted, perhaps as a codependent. Remember, the codependent pattern grows and strengthens if left alone. You may be able to stop the addiction process and begin your own recovery if you too adopt a spiritual strategy.

The methods are the same. A twelve-step process or something much like it is necessary. Remember, Christ is not the answer for you personally if you just say the words and do not surrender your addictions. The salvation process is not an automatic guarantee of cure from any disability or malfunction, including addiction/codependence. You too would do well to seek out a spiritual believer, preferably a counselor with preparation in dealing with addiction/codependence.

It is my belief that God wants you to be blessed. In Christ, God has blessings enough for you, and He awaits your spiritual move toward recovery. As you surrender those less than spiritual aspects of yourself, I believe God will bless those strong and worthwhile characteristics you possess as a child of the kingdom of God.

I believe God wants you to have access to a spiritual relationship of intimacy. I believe God wants you to maintain an awareness of the very presence of God each day. I believe God wants you to grow and develop in all aspects of your person, including your spiritual self, as you move continuously in recovery.

I would hope that you have a Christian foundation as you begin your spiritual journey. If not, then I hope that you will be open to the divine Spirit. Then as the Spirit of God leads, perhaps you will be led to the Spirit of Jesus Christ.

So, What Will Become of Codependency?

Codependence has provided a very valuable service to all of us. It will remain a way to communicate about one major way in which we become people with low self-esteem. It will be a way for us to understand how people who live closely together come to enrage or enslave each other emotionally when to those on the outside it looks as if the master is really the slave.

Codependence will be an important segment of training for counselors of many disciplines for many years to come. It will be an important issue for therapists of all fields to discover and find help for their own codependency. Then as they work directly with consumers they will not cause more difficulty than they cure in the lives of those who come to them for help.

Codependence is in an early stage of scientific research. Much careful statistical investigation, validation activities, and reflective reporting is yet to be done. Some scholars from within the codependency field will emerge to compare and contrast the findings of colleagues with similar scholars of other disciplines. Hopefully, there will be fewer theoretical and popular books available until there are more solid books in the field to establish its legitimacy as an independent discipline. Otherwise, codependency might be fragmented and its findings may quite well be usurped and scattered into a wide variety of other fields.

Many persons will be aided and assisted by this material, especially those who take seriously the challenge to receive therapy and establish recovery plans for the long term. Additional numbers of therapists will become more knowledgeable of its insights, its strategies, and begin to refine methodologies to make its helping values more available to the general public.

Knowledgeable ministers in local churches will use some of the materials for study among church members. Perhaps there will be a major growth of twelve-step program chapters to begin meeting within churches. Perhaps counseling centers within the churches or agencies of the churches will establish sharing groups or contract with fully qualified pastoral counselors or other appropriate professionals to establish therapy groups within the churches for children and/or adults.

And, perhaps the cure and prevention activities of the combined professions will be sufficiently successful that clusters of healthier families will emerge. The intensive need for codependency education and therapy may abate in time. That is my hope!

So, What Will Become of Christianity?

Christianity will be enriched by codependency education and therapy.

It has been a long time since a secular discipline has designed a remedial program that parallels the church's approach to the problems of life so closely.

- Both Christianity and codependency insist the major problem of the human condition is idolatry/addiction and that it has infected everyone.
- Both Christianity and codependency insist the way to recover from idolatry/addiction cannot be found within humans alone.
- Both Christianity and codependency insist the only cure for the human condition is a spiritual one and must begin with the codependent's choice of faith in God.
- Both Christianity and codependency insist the only cure for the human condition requires surrender to the will of God.
- Both Christianity and codependency insist the only cure for the human condition is to make a list of your sins against God and other people.
- Both Christianity and codependency insist the only cure for the human condition includes confessing your sins to God (and the codependents insist on the new believer confessing to at least one human being as well).
- Both Christianity and codependency insist the only recovery route for the human condition is to pray constantly to God for

the purpose of seeking God's will daily and for the power to carry out God's will.

●Both Christianity and codependency insist the only possible relief for the human condition is the above plan. The believer is then encouraged to seek out other unbelievers vigorously and seek to turn them away from their idolatries/addictions to a life of spirituality.

Now I grant you, that outline is a rather loose interpretation, but the parallel comparison is found in Acts 17:16-34. To find any group of persons who agree on the spiritual nature of life is to find a potential open doorway through which to make a clear Christian testimony. Many persons relating to a God-as-we-understand-Him are relating to an unknown God much as the Greeks to whom Paul spoke in Athens. It is constantly the joy of a Christian witness to find the Holy Spirit of God has gone before you to make the way ready for conversations about spiritual things. With many nonbelieving codependents with whom I have talked, this has been the case.

Also remember, codependent persons have been battered, beaten, abused, subjected to injustices at the individual, family, institutional, and societal levels. I call on the church and its members to listen to their cries of anguish, agony, and raw pain. As long as the churches can meet them as human brothers and sisters seeking God, as long as we offer them the open acceptance of Jesus Christ, the Lord of the cross who died for them and who accepts them unconditionally in love, as long as we are faithful to the New Testament, they will have spiritual friends with whom to touch base and accompany them in their paths of recovery.

Just so long as we can respond to their open inquiries and introduce them to the risen, living Christ, they will continue to find the hope of the gospel. If we try to rush them into our ways of doing church, we may frighten them. If we attempt to usher them from a pattern of never having been in church into the normal run of regular and special events of busy local church life too quickly, we may win them to faith in Christ and fail them in the task of discipling them into a lifetime of growing in the Spirit.

But a special word for Christian codependents.

Codependency is a real life problem. It will not go away and stay away by itself. It requires constant personal prayer and openness to God throughout every day. It probably will require that special jump start available through some counseling. It will be so much easier to maintain a recovery plan with a prayer partner or soul friend with whom you meet to talk, to pray, to read or discuss Scripture and other spiritually inspiring writings together, and with whom you share your process of recovery. Your prayers for each other may mean the difference between the old horrors of loneliness and knowing God is really intimate because you have found one of God's servants whose representation of God is worthy of the rank of ambassador.

Christianity will survive.

Codependents and addicts will continually be produced by our culture and require our loving attention. Many will continue to die with their spiritual parts still asleep.

Other codependents will enter a phase of spiritual life, and some of them will be in the churches of our Lord Jesus Christ.

My hope and prayer is that their new life will flourish, and the life of the churches will move ahead without hindrance to include them and their new spiritual vitality, a vitality we need and want without apology.

Sources of Assistance

Alcoholics Anonymous World Services
468 Park Avenue South
New York, New York 10016
(212) 686-1100

This national number is given for your information and in case you cannot find a local chapter of a twelve-step group.

Alcoholics Anonymous is also usually listed in local telephone directories as AA Alcoholics Anonymous. They maintain a list of most affiliated twelve-step recovery programs including the dates, times, and places of local meetings. They will also instruct you concerning the closed meeting and protect their anonymity. The person answering the phone at your local office may be able to give you information about how to contact leaders, sponsors, or others who may place you on a membership track of such an organization if you are interested.

Other national offices of interest are as follows:

Al-Anon/Alateen Family Group Headquarters
Madison Square Station
New York, New York 10010
(212) 683-1771

National Association for Children of Alcoholics
31706 Coast Highway, Suite 201
South Laguna, California 92677
(714) 499-3889

National Clearinghouse for Alcohol Information
P.O. Box 1908
Rockville, Maryland 20850
(301) 468-2600

The following is a listing of typical twelve-step groups likely to be meeting in large metropolitan areas in the United States. In the absence of an area listing of Alcoholics Anonymous or if the local AA chapter does not have a very complete listing of groups and group meetings, you may wish to contact a local mental health center for assistance.

Gamblers Anonymous	Al-Anon
Debtors Anonymous	Alateen
Smokers Anonymous	Parents Anonymous
Child Abusers Anonymous	Bulimics/Anorexics Anonymous
Shoplifters Anonymous	Adult Children of Alcoholics
Emotions Anonymous	Workaholics Anonymous
Sex Addicts Anonymous	Narcotics Anonymous

Bibliography

Ackerman, Robert. *Let Go and Grow: Recovery for Adult Children.* Deerfield Beach, Fla.: Health Communications, Inc., n.d.

Alcoholics Anonymous: The Story of How Many Thousands of Men and Women Have Recovered from Alcoholism. 3d ed. New York: Alcoholics Anonymous World Services, Inc., 1976.

* Beattie, Melody. *Codependent No More: How to Stop Controlling Others and Start Caring for Yourself.* New York: Harper and Row, 1987.

Booth, Leo. *Breaking the Chains: Understanding Religious Addiction and Religious Abuse.* Long Beach, Calif.: Emmaus Publications, 1989.

Bradshaw, John. *Healing the Shame That Binds You.* Deerfield Beach, Fla.: Health Communications, Inc., 1988.

Bratton, Mary. *A Guide to Family Intervention.* Pompano Beach, Fla.: Health Communications, Inc., 1987.

Brown, Stephanie. *Treating the Alcoholic.* New York: John Wiley and Sons, 1985.

Castine, Jacqueline. *Recovery from Rescuing.* Deerfield Beach, Fla.: Health Communications, Inc., 1989.

Cermak, Timmen L. *Diagnosing and Treating Co-Dependence.* Minneapolis: Johnson Institute, 1986.

Clinebell, Howard. *Understanding and Counseling the Alcoholic: Through Religion and Psychology.* Nashville: Abingdon Press, 1956.

Co-Dependency: An Emerging Issue. Pompano Beach, Fla.: Health Communications, Inc., 1984.

* Conver, Christopher C. and Leigh E. Conver. *Self-Defeating Life-Styles*. Nashville: Broadman Press, 1988.

Covington, Stephanie and Liana Beckett. *Leaving the Enchanted Forest: The Path from Relationship Addiction to Intimacy*. San Francisco: Harper and Row, 1988.

Friel, John C. and Linda D. Friel. *Adult Children: The Secrets of Dysfunctional Families*. Deerfield Beach, Fla.: Health Communications, Inc., 1988.

Gallant, Donald M. *Alcoholism: A Guide to Diagnosis, Intervention, and Treatment*. New York: W. W. Norton and Company, 1987.

Gravitz, Herbert L. and Julie D. Bowden. *A Guide for Adult Children of Alcoholics*. New York: Simon and Schuster, 1985.

* Johnson, Vernon E. *Intervention: How To Help Someone Who Doesn't Want Help, A Step-by-Step Guide for Families and Friends of Chemically Dependent Persons*. Minneapolis: Johnson Institute, n.d.

Larson, Ernie. *Basics of Co-Dependency*. Brooklyn Park, N. Mex.: E. Larson Enterprises, 1983.

Ludwig, Arnold M. *Understanding the Alcoholic's Mind: The Nature of Craving and How to Control It*. New York: Oxford University Press, 1988.

* Martin, Sara Hines. *Healing for Adult Children of Alcoholics*. Nashville: Broadman Press, 1988.

* May. Gerald G. *Addiction and Grace*. San Francisco: Harper and Row, 1988.

McCormick, Patrick. *Sin As Addiction*. New York: Paulist Press, 1989.

Missildine, W. Hugh. *Your Inner Child of the Past*. New York: Simon and Schuster, 1963.

    * Nakken, Craig. *The Addictive Personality: Understanding Compulsion in Our Lives*. San Francisco: Harper and Row, 1988.

* Oates, Wayne E. *Alcohol: In and Out of the Church*. Nashville: Broadman Press, 1966.

* _____. *On Becoming the Children of God*. Philadelphia: The Westminster Press, 1969.

_____. *The Presence of God in Pastoral Counseling*. Waco:

Word Books, 1986.

_____. *The Religious Care of the Psychiatric Patient.* Philadelphia: The Westminster Press, 1978.

_____. *When Religion Gets Sick.* Philadelphia: The Westminster Press, 1970.

* Schaef, Anne Wilson. *Co-Dependence: Misunderstood, Mistreated.* Minneapolis: Winston Press, 1985.

_____. *Women's Reality: An Emerging Female System in the White Male Society.* Minneapolis: Winston Press, 1981.

Subby, Robert. *Lost in the Shuffle: The Co-Dependent Reality.* Pompano Beach, Fla.: Health Communications, Inc., 1987.

Vaughn, Joe. *Family Intervention: Hope for Families Struggling with Alcohol and Drugs.* Louisville: Westminster/John Knox, 1989.

Wegscheider-Cruse, Sharon. *Choicemaking.* Pompano Beach, Fla.: Health Communications, Inc., 1985.

_____. *Learning To Love Yourself: Finding Your Self-Worth.* Deerfield Beach, Fla.: Health Communications, Inc., 1987.

Weiss, Laurie and Jonathan B. Weiss. *Recovery from Co-Dependency: It's Never Too Late to Reclaim Your Childhood.* Deerfield Beach, Fla.: Health Communications, Inc., 1989.

Why Haven't I Been Able to Help? rev. ed. Minneapolis: Johnson Institute, n.d.

Woititz, Janet Geringer. *Adult Children of Alcoholics.* Pompano Beach, Fla.: Health Communications, Inc., 1983.

_____. *Home Away from Home.* Pompano Beach, Fla.: Health Communications, Inc., 1987.

_____. *Struggle for Intimacy.* Pompano Beach, Fla.: Health Communications, Inc., 1985.

* Woodruff, C. Roy. *Alcoholism and Christian Experience.* Philadelphia: The Westminster Press, 1968.

* Suggested readings to begin additional reading.